Preface

Welcome to "Mastering Apache Maven," a comprehensive guide designed to help you understand and leverage the powerful capabilities of Apache Maven for your software projects. Whether you are a novice or an experienced developer, this book aims to provide you with the knowledge and tools you need to effectively manage your builds, dependencies, and project lifecycles using Maven.

This book is unique in that it was entirely generated by an artificial intelligence, which I believe to be a domain expert in the field. The content herein was crafted to provide clear, concise, and accurate information about Apache Maven, ensuring that you have access to the best practices and insights available.

Why Apache Maven?

Apache Maven is a cornerstone in the world of Java development and beyond. Its ability to streamline the build process, manage project dependencies, and maintain consistency across multiple projects makes it an invaluable tool for developers. This book covers all aspects of Maven, from basic setup and configuration to advanced topics such as plugin development and continuous integration.

What You Will Learn

Throughout this book, you will find detailed explanations and practical examples that will guide you through the following key areas:

1. **Introduction to Apache Maven**: Gain a foundational understanding of what Maven is and how it can benefit your projects.
2. **Building Projects with Apache Maven**: Learn how to configure and manage the Project Object Model (POM), build and package projects, and manage dependencies.

3. **Working with Maven Plugins**: Discover how to use built-in plugins, create custom plugins, and configure them for your specific needs.
4. **Managing Dependencies with Maven**: Understand the importance of dependency management and how Maven handles it.
5. **Working with Maven Repositories**: Explore the structure and configuration of local and remote repositories, and learn how to publish artifacts.
6. **Managing Builds with Maven**: Delve into the Maven build lifecycle, customize builds, and integrate Maven with continuous integration tools.
7. **Testing with Apache Maven**: Learn how to set up and run unit and integration tests, and analyze code coverage and quality.
8. **Advanced Maven Concepts**: Master multi-module projects, manage project releases, and use Maven with Java EE applications.

The Role of AI in Crafting This Book

The entire content of this book was generated by artificial intelligence, which has been trained on a vast corpus of programming and technical literature. This AI-driven approach ensures that the information presented is both comprehensive and up-to-date, reflecting the latest trends and best practices in the industry. As the author, I have overseen this process to ensure that the generated content meets the highest standards of quality and relevance.

Who Should Read This Book?

This book is intended for software developers, build engineers, and project managers who are involved in the development and maintenance of software projects using Apache Maven. Whether you are just starting with Maven or looking to deepen your understanding, this book provides the knowledge and insights needed to excel.

Acknowledgements

I would like to extend my gratitude to the developers and maintainers of Apache Maven for creating such a robust and versatile tool. Additionally, I appreciate the advancements in AI technology that made the generation of this book possible.

Thank you for choosing this book as your guide to mastering Apache Maven. I hope it serves you well in your journey to becoming a proficient and efficient developer.

1 Introduction to Apache Maven

1.1 What is Apache Maven?

Apache Maven is a powerful build automation and project management tool that is widely used in the software development industry. It provides a comprehensive and standardized way to manage projects, build software, and handle dependencies. Maven is built on the concept of a project object model (POM), which is an XML file that describes the structure and configuration of a project.

1.1.1 Key Features of Apache Maven

Apache Maven offers several key features that make it a popular choice among developers and organizations:

1. Dependency Management

One of the core features of Maven is its ability to manage project dependencies. Maven simplifies the process of including external libraries and frameworks in your project by automatically downloading and managing the required dependencies. It maintains a central repository of dependencies, making it easy to add, update, and remove dependencies as needed.

2. Build Automation

Maven provides a robust and flexible build system that automates the process of compiling source code, running tests, packaging the application, and generating documentation. It follows a convention-over-configuration approach, which means that it provides sensible defaults for most build tasks, reducing the need for manual configuration.

3. Project Structure and Standardization

Maven enforces a standardized project structure, which helps in maintaining consistency across different projects and makes it easier for developers to understand and navigate the codebase. The predefined directory structure separates source code, resources, and test code, making it easier to organize and manage project files.

4. Plugin System

Maven has a rich ecosystem of plugins that extend its functionality and allow developers to perform a wide range of tasks. Plugins can be used to compile code, run tests, generate reports, deploy artifacts, and perform various other build-related activities. Maven plugins are highly configurable and can be easily integrated into the build process.

5. Reproducible Builds

Maven ensures that builds are reproducible by using a declarative approach to define the build process. The POM file specifies the project's dependencies, build steps, and other configuration details, making it easy to recreate the build environment on different machines. This helps in achieving consistent and predictable build results across different development and deployment environments.

1.1.2 Benefits of Using Apache Maven

Using Apache Maven offers several benefits to developers and organizations:

1. Simplified Project Setup

Maven simplifies the process of setting up a new project by providing a standard project structure and predefined build lifecycle. Developers can quickly get started with a new project without spending time on manual configuration.

2. Dependency Management

Maven's dependency management feature eliminates the need for manually downloading and managing external libraries. It automatically resolves and downloads the required dependencies from remote repositories, ensuring that the project always has the correct versions of the dependencies.

3. Build Consistency

By enforcing a standardized project structure and build process, Maven ensures consistency across different projects within an organization. This makes it easier for developers to switch between projects and reduces the learning curve for new team members.

4. Continuous Integration and Deployment

Maven integrates seamlessly with popular continuous integration (CI) tools like Jenkins, allowing for automated builds, tests, and deployments. This enables organizations to adopt a continuous integration and delivery (CI/CD) approach, improving development efficiency and reducing time to market.

5. Extensibility

Maven's plugin system allows developers to extend its functionality and customize the build process to suit their specific requirements. Developers can create custom plugins or leverage existing plugins from the Maven ecosystem to perform complex build tasks.

6. Community Support

Apache Maven has a large and active community of developers who contribute to its development and provide support through forums, mailing lists, and online resources. This community-driven approach ensures that Maven remains up-to-date, reliable, and well-documented.

In conclusion, Apache Maven is a powerful and widely-used build automation and project management tool. It simplifies the process of managing dependencies, automates the build process, enforces project structure and standardization, and provides extensibility through its plugin system. By using Maven, developers and organizations can benefit from simplified project setup, improved build consistency, efficient dependency management, and seamless integration with CI/CD pipelines.

1.2 Installing Apache Maven

Installing Apache Maven is a straightforward process that allows you to quickly set up and start using this powerful build automation tool. In this section, we will guide you through the steps required to install Apache Maven on your system.

1.2.1 Prerequisites

Before installing Apache Maven, ensure that your system meets the following prerequisites:

1. Java Development Kit (JDK): Apache Maven requires a JDK to run. Make sure you have a compatible JDK installed on your system. You can check if Java is installed by opening a terminal or command prompt and running the command `java -version`. If Java is not installed, download and install the latest JDK from the official Oracle website.

2. System Requirements: Apache Maven is a Java-based tool and can run on various operating systems, including Windows, macOS, and Linux. Ensure that your system meets the minimum requirements specified by the JDK and the operating system.

1.2.2 Downloading Apache Maven

To download Apache Maven, follow these steps:

1. Open your web browser and navigate to the official Apache Maven website at **https://maven.apache.org**.

2. On the homepage, locate the "Download" section and click on the link to access the download page.

3. On the download page, you will find the latest stable release of Apache Maven. Click on the link to download the binary zip file.

4. Once the download is complete, extract the contents of the zip file to a directory of your choice. This directory will be referred to as the "Maven installation directory" throughout this book.

1.2.3 Configuring Environment Variables

To use Apache Maven from the command line, you need to configure the appropriate environment variables. Follow these steps to set up the environment variables:

Windows

1. Open the Control Panel and navigate to System and Security > System > Advanced system settings.

2. In the System Properties window, click on the "Environment Variables" button.

3. In the "System Variables" section, scroll down and locate the "Path" variable. Select it and click on the "Edit" button.

4. In the "Edit Environment Variable" window, click on the "New" button and add the path to the Maven installation directory. For example, if you extracted Maven to `C:\apache-maven`, add `C:\apache-maven\bin` to the "Path" variable.

5. Click "OK" to save the changes.

macOS and Linux

1. Open a terminal window.

2. Run the following command to open the `.bash_profile` file in a text editor:

```
nano ~/.bash_profile
```

3. Add the following line to the file, replacing `/path/to/maven` with the actual path to the Maven installation directory:

```
export PATH=/path/to/maven/bin:$PATH
```

4. Press `Ctrl + X` to exit the text editor, and when prompted to save the changes, press *Y* and then `Enter`.

5. Run the following command to apply the changes:

```
source ~/.bash_profile
```

1.2.4 Verifying the Installation

To verify that Apache Maven is installed correctly, open a terminal or command prompt and run the following command:

```
mvn --version
```

If Maven is installed properly, you should see the version information and other details displayed on the screen.

Congratulations! You have successfully installed Apache Maven on your system. In the next section, we will explore how to create a Maven project and get started with building projects using Maven.

1.3 Creating a Maven Project

Creating a Maven project is a straightforward process that allows you to quickly set up a project structure and manage its dependencies. In this section, we will explore the steps involved in creating a Maven project and understand the various components of a Maven project.

1.3.1 Setting Up the Project

To create a Maven project, you need to have Maven installed on your system. If you haven't installed Maven yet, refer to Chapter 1.2 for instructions on how to install it.

Once Maven is installed, open your terminal or command prompt and navigate to the directory where you want to create your project. Then, run the following command:

```
mvn archetype:generate
```

This command will prompt you to choose an archetype, which is a template for creating a project. Maven provides several archetypes for different types of projects, such as Java applications, web applications, and more. You can select the archetype that best suits your project requirements.

1.3.2 Choosing an Archetype

When prompted to choose an archetype, you will see a list of available archetypes along with their corresponding numbers. Enter the number of the archetype you want to use and press Enter. Maven will then ask you to provide a groupId, artifactId, and version for your project.

- **groupId**: The groupId identifies your project uniquely across all projects. It usually follows the reverse domain name convention, such as com.example.

- **artifactId**: The artifactId is the name of your project. It should be descriptive and meaningful.
- **version**: The version represents the version of your project. It is recommended to use the default value provided by Maven.

After providing the required information, Maven will create the project structure based on the chosen archetype and generate the necessary files.

1.3.3 Understanding the Project Structure

Once the project is created, let's take a closer look at the generated project structure. By default, Maven follows a standard directory structure that helps organize your project's source code, resources, and other files.

Here is an overview of the main directories and files in a Maven project:

- **src/main/java**: This directory contains the Java source code files of your project.
- **src/main/resources**: This directory is used to store non-Java resources, such as configuration files, properties files, and XML files.
- **src/test/java**: This directory contains the test source code files for your project.
- **src/test/resources**: This directory is used to store test-specific resources.
- **pom.xml**: The pom.xml file is the heart of a Maven project. It is an XML file that defines the project's configuration, dependencies, and build settings.

Apart from these directories, Maven also generates some additional files and directories based on the archetype you chose. These files and directories may include web application-specific files, configuration files, and more.

1.3.4 Modifying the Project Configuration

After creating a Maven project, you can modify its configuration by editing the pom.xml file. The pom.xml file contains various sections, such as project information, dependencies, build settings, and more.

To add dependencies to your project, you can specify them in the dependencies section of the pom.xml file. Maven will automatically download and manage the required dependencies for your project.

You can also configure the build settings in the pom.xml file. For example, you can specify the source and target Java versions, configure plugins, define build profiles, and more.

1.3.5 Building the Project

Once you have set up your Maven project and made the necessary modifications to the pom.xml file, you can build the project using the following command:

```
mvn clean install
```

This command will compile the source code, run tests, package the project, and install it in your local Maven repository. The resulting artifact can then be used by other projects as a dependency.

1.3.6 Importing the Project into an IDE

If you prefer to work with an Integrated Development Environment (IDE), you can import your Maven project into your IDE of choice. Most popular IDEs, such as Eclipse, IntelliJ IDEA, and NetBeans, have built-in support for Maven.

To import the project, open your IDE and choose the option to import an existing Maven project. Select the root directory of your project and let the IDE handle the rest. It will automatically recognize the project structure and configure the necessary settings.

Importing the project into an IDE allows you to take advantage of features like code completion, debugging, and build automation provided by the IDE.

Congratulations! You have successfully created a Maven project and learned about its structure and configuration. In the next section, we will dive deeper into configuring the Project Object Model (POM) and explore various build options provided by Maven.

1.4 Understanding the Maven Directory Structure

The directory structure of a Maven project is an essential aspect of understanding how Maven organizes and manages projects. By following a specific directory structure, Maven can effectively build, package, and deploy projects. In this section, we will explore the standard Maven directory structure and discuss the purpose of each directory.

1.4.1 The Project Root Directory

At the root level of a Maven project, you will find the project's main directory. This directory serves as the starting point for the entire project and contains various configuration files and subdirectories. The project root directory typically has the same name as the project itself.

1.4.2 The src Directory

The `src` directory is where you store the source code of your project. It contains two main subdirectories: *`main`* and `test`.

1.4.2.1 The main Directory

The *`main`* directory is where you place the main source code of your project. It contains the following subdirectories:

- *`java`*: This directory is used to store the Java source code files of your project. By convention, the package structure of your Java classes should mirror the directory structure within the *`java`* directory.
- *`resources`*: This directory is used to store non-Java resources, such as configuration files, property files, XML files, and other resources required by your project. The

resources within this directory are typically included in the project's final artifact.

1.4.2.2 The test Directory

The *test* directory is where you place the test source code of your project. It follows a similar structure to the *main* directory and contains the following subdirectories:

- *java*: This directory is used to store the test source code files. Just like the *main/java* directory, the package structure of your test classes should mirror the directory structure within the *test/java* directory.
- *resources*: This directory is used to store test-specific resources, such as test configuration files or test data files. These resources are only used during the execution of tests and are not included in the project's final artifact.

1.4.3 The target Directory

The *target* directory is where Maven places the output of the build process. It contains the compiled classes, packaged artifacts, and other generated files. The contents of the *target* directory are temporary and can be safely deleted without affecting the project's source code.

1.4.4 The pom.xml File

The *pom.xml* file is the heart of a Maven project. It is an XML file that contains the project's configuration, dependencies, build instructions, and other essential information. The *pom.xml* file is located in the project's root directory and is used by Maven to build and manage the project.

1.4.5 The .m2 Directory

The *.m2* directory is the local repository where Maven stores all the downloaded dependencies. It is located in the user's home directory and is automatically created by Maven if it doesn't exist. The *.m2* directory is crucial for offline development, as it allows Maven to resolve dependencies without an internet connection.

1.4.6 Other Directories

Apart from the main directories mentioned above, a Maven project may also contain additional directories based on its specific requirements. Some common additional directories include:

- *bin*: This directory is used to store executable scripts or binaries related to the project.
- *docs*: This directory is used to store project documentation, such as user manuals, API documentation, or design documents.
- *lib*: This directory is used to store external libraries or dependencies that are not available in a public repository.
- *webapp*: This directory is used in web application projects and contains web-related resources, such as HTML, CSS, JavaScript, and JSP files.

It's important to note that while Maven provides a standard directory structure, it is also highly customizable. You can modify the directory structure to suit your project's specific needs by configuring the appropriate settings in the *pom.xml* file.

Understanding the Maven directory structure is crucial for effectively organizing and managing your projects. By adhering to the standard structure, you can ensure that your project is easily maintainable, scalable, and compatible with other Maven-based projects.

2 Building Projects with Apache Maven

2.1 Configuring the Project Object Model (POM)

The Project Object Model (POM) is the fundamental building block of Apache Maven. It is an XML file that contains information about the project and configuration details used by Maven to build the project. The POM serves as the blueprint for the project, defining its structure, dependencies, and build process.

2.1.1 Understanding the POM Structure

The POM file is named *pom.xml* and is located in the root directory of the project. It follows a hierarchical structure, with various elements and properties that define the project's characteristics. Let's take a closer look at the important elements of the POM:

2.1.1.1 Project Information

The *<groupId>*, *<artifactId>*, and *<version>* elements are used to uniquely identify the project. The *<groupId>* represents the group or organization that the project belongs to, while the *<artifactId>* is the unique name of the project. The *<version>* specifies the version of the project.

```
<groupId>com.example</groupId>
<artifactId>my-project</artifactId>
<version>1.0.0</version>
```

2.1.1.2 Project Dependencies

The *<dependencies>* element is used to declare the dependencies required by the project. Dependencies are external libraries or modules that the project relies on to function correctly. Maven automatically downloads and manages these dependencies, ensuring that the project has access to the required libraries during the build process.

```
<dependencies>
  <dependency>
    <groupId>org.springframework</groupId>
    <artifactId>spring-core</artifactId>
    <version>5.2.0</version>
  </dependency>
  <dependency>
    <groupId>com.google.guava</groupId>
    <artifactId>guava</artifactId>
    <version>30.0-jre</version>
  </dependency>
</dependencies>
```

2.1.1.3 Build Configuration

The *<build>* element contains configuration details related to the build process. It allows you to customize various aspects of the build, such as the source directory, output directory, and plugins to be used. Maven provides a set of default build phases and goals, but you can override or extend them as needed.

```
<build>
  <sourceDirectory>src/main/java</sourceDirectory>
  <outputDirectory>target/classes</outputDirectory>
  <plugins>
    <plugin>
      <groupId>org.apache.maven.plugins</groupId>
      <artifactId>maven-compiler-plugin</artifactId>
      <version>3.8.1</version>
      <configuration>
        <source>1.8</source>
        <target>1.8</target>
      </configuration>
    </plugin>
  </plugins>
</build>
```

2.1.2 Inheriting from Parent POM

Maven allows projects to inherit configuration from a parent POM. This promotes consistency and reduces duplication across multiple projects within an organization. By defining a parent POM, you can centralize common configuration settings and dependencies, which are automatically inherited by the child projects.

To inherit from a parent POM, you need to specify the parent's coordinates in the *<parent>* element of the child POM. Maven will then merge the child POM with the parent POM, combining their configurations.

```
<parent>
  <groupId>com.example</groupId>
  <artifactId>parent-project</artifactId>
  <version>1.0.0</version>
</parent>
```

2.1.3 Overriding POM Configuration

While inheriting from a parent POM provides a convenient way to reuse configuration, you may need to override certain settings in the child project. Maven allows you to override inherited configuration by specifying the desired values in the child POM.

For example, if the parent POM sets the source directory to *src/main/java*, but you want to use a different directory for the child project, you can override it as follows:

```
<build>
  <sourceDirectory>src/main/custom</sourceDirectory>
</build>
```

2.1.4 Building the Project with Maven

Once the POM is properly configured, you can build the project using Maven. Open a command prompt or terminal, navigate to the project's root directory (where the *pom.xml* file is located), and run the following command:

```
mvn clean install
```

This command triggers the Maven build process, which compiles the source code, runs tests, and packages the project into a distributable format (e.g., JAR, WAR). The *clean* goal ensures that any existing build artifacts are removed before starting the build.

2.1.5 Understanding POM Inheritance and Aggregation

In addition to inheriting configuration from a parent POM, Maven also supports POM aggregation. Aggregation allows you to create a multi-module project where each module has its own POM, and a parent POM aggregates the modules together.

By defining a parent POM for a multi-module project, you can manage the build process and dependencies across all modules from a single location. This simplifies the management of large projects with multiple interconnected modules.

2.1.6 Summary

In this section, we explored the Project Object Model (POM) and its role in configuring Apache Maven projects. We discussed the structure of the POM, including project information, dependencies, and build configuration. We also learned about inheriting from a parent POM, overriding configuration, and building the project with Maven. Understanding the POM is crucial for effectively managing and building projects with Apache Maven.

2.2 Building and Packaging Projects

Building and packaging projects is a fundamental aspect of Apache Maven. In this section, we will explore the various features and capabilities of Maven that enable developers to efficiently build and package their projects.

2.2.1 Understanding the Build Process

Before diving into the details of building and packaging projects with Maven, it is essential to understand the overall build process. Maven follows a convention-over-configuration approach, which means that it provides a predefined structure and set of conventions for organizing projects. This structure allows Maven to automatically handle many aspects of the build process, such as compiling source code, running tests, and packaging the project into a distributable format.

At the heart of Maven's build process is the Project Object Model (POM). The POM is an XML file that describes the project's configuration, dependencies, and build settings. It serves as the central configuration file for Maven and provides a blueprint for building the project.

2.2.2 Configuring the Build

To configure the build process, developers need to modify the POM file. The POM contains various sections, such as project information, dependencies, build plugins, and profiles. These sections allow developers to define the project's characteristics and customize the build process according to their requirements.

One of the essential sections in the POM is the *<build>* section. This section allows developers to specify the build plugins and goals that Maven should execute during the build process. Build plugins are responsible for performing specific tasks, such as compiling source code, running tests, generating documentation, and packaging the project.

Maven provides a wide range of built-in plugins that cover most common build tasks. These plugins can be easily configured and customized to suit the project's needs. Additionally, developers can also create their custom plugins to extend Maven's functionality further.

2.2.3 Building the Project

To build a Maven project, developers need to execute the *mvn* command followed by the desired build goal. Maven supports various build goals, such as *clean*, *compile*, *test*, *package*, and *install*. Each goal represents a specific phase in the build lifecycle.

The build lifecycle consists of a sequence of phases, and each phase represents a specific step in the build process. For example, the *compile* phase compiles the project's source code, the *test* phase runs the project's unit tests, and the *package* phase packages the project into a distributable format, such as a JAR or WAR file.

By default, Maven executes all the phases up to and including the specified goal. For example, if the *package* goal is executed, Maven will automatically execute the preceding phases, such as *compile* and *test*. This ensures that the project is built correctly and all necessary steps are performed.

2.2.4 Packaging the Project

Packaging the project is the final step in the build process. Maven supports various packaging formats, such as JAR, WAR, and EAR. The packaging format is specified in the POM file using the *<packaging>* element.

When the project is packaged, Maven creates an artifact that can be easily distributed and deployed. The artifact contains the compiled code, resources, and other necessary files. Maven also generates a unique version number for each artifact, allowing developers to track and manage different versions of the project.

Maven provides a convenient way to package the project using the *package* goal. When this goal is executed, Maven performs all the necessary steps to compile the code, run tests, and package the project into the specified format. The resulting artifact is then stored in the project's target directory.

2.2.5 Customizing the Build

Maven allows developers to customize the build process by configuring various build plugins and settings. By modifying the POM file, developers can add or remove build plugins, specify custom build goals, and configure the build environment.

For example, developers can configure the *maven-compiler-plugin* to specify the Java version to use during compilation. They can also configure the *maven-surefire-plugin* to customize the behavior of the test execution, such as excluding specific tests or generating test reports.

Additionally, Maven supports the use of profiles, which allow developers to define different build configurations for different environments or scenarios. Profiles can be activated based on various conditions, such as the operating system, the presence of specific files, or the value of system properties. This flexibility enables developers to create build configurations that are tailored to specific requirements.

2.2.6 Summary

In this section, we explored the process of building and packaging projects with Apache Maven. We learned about the build lifecycle, the role of the POM file in configuring the build, and the various build goals and phases. We also discussed how Maven allows developers to customize the build process by configuring build plugins and settings. By understanding these concepts, developers can effectively utilize Maven to build and package their projects in a consistent and efficient manner.

2.3 Managing Dependencies with Maven

One of the key features of Apache Maven is its ability to manage dependencies in a project. In software development, dependencies refer to external libraries or modules that are required for a project to function properly. Managing dependencies manually can be a complex and time-consuming task, especially in large projects with multiple dependencies. Maven simplifies this process by providing a centralized and automated way to handle dependencies.

2.3.1 Declaring Dependencies in the POM

In Maven, dependencies are declared in the Project Object Model (POM) file, which is an XML file that describes the project and its configuration. The POM file serves as the central configuration file for a Maven project and contains information such as project name, version, and dependencies.

To declare a dependency in the POM file, you need to specify the group ID, artifact ID, and version of the dependency. The group ID represents the organization or group that created the dependency, the artifact ID is the name of the dependency, and the version indicates the specific version of the dependency that should be used.

Here is an example of how a dependency is declared in the POM file:

```
<dependencies>
  <dependency>
    <groupId>com.example</groupId>
    <artifactId>my-library</artifactId>
    <version>1.0.0</version>
  </dependency>
</dependencies>
```

In this example, the project has a dependency on a library called "my-library" with a version of "1.0.0" and a group ID of "com.example". Maven will automatically download the required library from a remote repository and include it in the project's classpath.

2.3.2 Resolving Dependencies

Once the dependencies are declared in the POM file, Maven takes care of resolving and downloading the required dependencies. Maven uses a concept called dependency resolution to determine the correct versions of the dependencies and retrieve them from the configured repositories.

When Maven encounters a dependency declaration, it first checks the local repository, which is a local cache of downloaded dependencies on the developer's machine. If the dependency is not found in the local repository, Maven searches the remote repositories specified in the POM file or the settings.xml file.

Maven follows a specific algorithm to resolve dependencies, taking into account factors such as version ranges, transitive dependencies, and conflicts. It ensures that the correct versions of the dependencies are downloaded and used in the project.

2.3.3 Managing Transitive Dependencies

One of the powerful features of Maven is its ability to manage transitive dependencies. Transitive dependencies are dependencies that are required by other dependencies. For example, if your project depends on library A, and library A depends on library B, Maven will automatically resolve and include both library A and library B in your project.

This automatic management of transitive dependencies greatly simplifies the process of managing complex projects with multiple dependencies. Maven handles the entire dependency tree, ensuring that all required dependencies are included and that there are no conflicts between different versions of the same dependency.

However, it is important to note that transitive dependencies can sometimes lead to conflicts or compatibility issues. If two dependencies have conflicting versions of the same library, Maven will try to resolve the conflict based on its dependency resolution algorithm. In some cases, manual intervention may be required to resolve conflicts or exclude certain transitive dependencies.

2.3.4 Dependency Scope

In addition to declaring dependencies, Maven allows you to specify the scope of a dependency. The scope determines how the dependency is used during different phases of the build process.

The most commonly used dependency scopes are:

- **compile**: This is the default scope and indicates that the dependency is required for compiling and running the project.
- **test**: Dependencies with this scope are only required for running tests and are not included in the final artifact.
- **provided**: Dependencies with this scope are required for compiling the project, but are expected to be provided by the runtime environment.
- **runtime**: Dependencies with this scope are required for running the project, but not for compiling it.
- **system**: Dependencies with this scope are similar to provided scope, but you have to provide the path to the dependency explicitly.

By specifying the appropriate scope for each dependency, you can control how they are used and included in the project.

2.3.5 Managing Dependency Versions

In Maven, it is common to use version ranges for dependencies to allow flexibility in selecting the appropriate version. Version ranges are specified using a combination of square brackets and parentheses.

For example, the following dependency declaration specifies a version range from 1.0.0 (inclusive) to 2.0.0 (exclusive):

```
<dependency>
  <groupId>com.example</groupId>
  <artifactId>my-library</artifactId>
  <version>[1.0.0,2.0.0)</version>
</dependency>
```

Maven will select the highest version within the specified range that is available in the configured repositories.

However, it is generally recommended to use specific versions for dependencies to ensure reproducibility and avoid unexpected behavior due to version updates. Using version ranges should be done with caution and only when necessary.

2.3.6 Excluding Dependencies

In some cases, you may need to exclude certain transitive dependencies that are automatically included by Maven. This can be done by specifying an exclusion in the dependency declaration.

Here is an example of excluding a transitive dependency:

```
<dependency>
  <groupId>com.example</groupId>
  <artifactId>my-library</artifactId>
  <version>1.0.0</version>
  <exclusions>
    <exclusion>
      <groupId>org.unwanted</groupId>
      <artifactId>unwanted-library</artifactId>
    </exclusion>
  </exclusions>
</dependency>
```

In this example, the unwanted-library dependency is excluded from the my-library dependency.

Exclusions are useful when you want to avoid conflicts or when you have a specific version requirement for a dependency.

In this section, we explored how Apache Maven simplifies the management of dependencies in a project. We learned how to declare dependencies in the POM file, resolve them from local and remote repositories, manage transitive dependencies, specify dependency scopes, handle dependency versions, and exclude unwanted dependencies. Maven's dependency management capabilities greatly enhance the efficiency and reliability of building and managing software projects.

2.4 Running Maven Build Lifecycle Phases

Once you have configured your Maven project and defined the necessary dependencies, it's time to build and package your project. Maven provides a build lifecycle that consists of a series of build phases, each responsible for a specific task in the build process. In this section, we will explore the different build lifecycle phases and how to run them.

2.4.1 Understanding the Maven Build Lifecycle

Before diving into running the build lifecycle phases, let's first understand the concept of the Maven build lifecycle. The Maven build lifecycle is a predefined sequence of phases that are executed in a specific order. Each phase represents a specific stage in the build process, such as compiling source code, running tests, packaging the project, and deploying artifacts.

The Maven build lifecycle consists of three main lifecycles: the default lifecycle, the clean lifecycle, and the site lifecycle. The default lifecycle is the most commonly used and includes phases such as validate, compile, test, package, install, and deploy. The clean lifecycle is responsible for cleaning the project by removing any generated files and artifacts. The site lifecycle is used for generating project documentation.

2.4.2 Running Build Lifecycle Phases

To run a specific build lifecycle phase, you can use the *mvn* command followed by the phase name. For example, to compile your project, you can run the following command:

```
mvn compile
```

This will execute the `compile` phase of the default lifecycle. Maven will automatically handle the dependencies and compile the source code.

If you want to run multiple phases, you can specify them in the command. For example, to compile and package your project, you can run:

```
mvn compile package
```

Maven will execute the *compile* phase followed by the *package* phase. This will compile the source code and package it into the desired format, such as a JAR or WAR file.

2.4.3 Skipping Build Lifecycle Phases

Sometimes, you may want to skip certain build lifecycle phases. Maven provides a way to skip phases using the *-Dmaven.test.skip* flag. For example, if you want to skip the test phase, you can run:

```
mvn package -Dmaven.test.skip=true
```

This will skip the execution of the test phase and proceed with the packaging phase. Skipping phases can be useful when you are in a hurry or when you want to focus on a specific part of the build process.

2.4.4 Specifying Build Profiles

Build profiles allow you to customize the build process based on different environments or requirements. Maven provides a way to activate specific profiles during the build. To activate a profile, you can use the *-P* flag followed by the profile name. For example, to activate a profile named “production”, you can run:

```
mvn package -P production
```

This will activate the "production" profile and execute any configuration or tasks associated with that profile. Profiles can be used to define different sets of dependencies, plugins, or build properties for different environments.

2.4.5 Skipping Tests during the Build

During the build process, you may want to skip the execution of tests. Maven provides a way to skip tests using the *-DskipTests* flag. For example, to skip tests during the package phase, you can run:

```
mvn package -DskipTests
```

This will skip the execution of tests and proceed with the packaging phase. Skipping tests can be useful when you are in a development phase and want to quickly build and package your project without running the tests.

2.4.6 Running Custom Build Lifecycle Phases

In addition to the predefined build lifecycle phases, Maven allows you to define your own custom phases. Custom phases can be useful when you have specific tasks that need to be executed as part of the build process. To define a custom phase, you need to create a plugin and bind it to the desired phase.

Once you have defined a custom phase, you can run it using the *mvn* command followed by the phase name. For example, if you have a custom phase named "generate-docs", you can run:

```
mvn generate-docs
```

This will execute the custom phase and perform the tasks associated with it. Custom phases can be used to automate tasks such as generating documentation, running code analysis, or performing code generation.

2.4.7 Understanding Build Lifecycle Ordering

The Maven build lifecycle follows a specific order of execution. Each phase depends on the successful completion of the previous phase. For example, the *compile* phase depends on the successful execution of the *validate* phase, and the *package* phase depends on the successful execution of the *compile* phase.

Understanding the build lifecycle ordering is important to ensure that the build process runs smoothly. If a phase fails, Maven will stop the build process and report the error. It's important to fix any errors before proceeding with the next phase.

2.4.8 Overriding Default Lifecycle Phases

In some cases, you may want to override the default behavior of a build lifecycle phase. Maven allows you to override default phases by binding custom plugins to those phases. This can be useful when you need to perform additional tasks or modify the behavior of a specific phase.

To override a default phase, you need to create a plugin and bind it to the desired phase. When Maven encounters the overridden phase, it will execute the custom plugin instead of the default behavior. This gives you the flexibility to customize the build process according to your project's requirements.

Conclusion

Running Maven build lifecycle phases is an essential part of building and packaging your projects. Understanding the different phases and how to run them allows you to automate the build process and ensure the successful completion of your projects. By leveraging the power of Maven, you can streamline your development workflow and focus on writing high-quality code.

3 Working with Maven Plugins

3.1 Introduction to Maven Plugins

Maven plugins are an essential part of Apache Maven, providing additional functionality and extending the capabilities of the build system. Plugins are used to perform various tasks during the build process, such as compiling source code, running tests, packaging the project, and deploying artifacts to repositories. In this section, we will explore the basics of Maven plugins, including their purpose, how to use built-in plugins, and how to create custom plugins.

Purpose of Maven Plugins

Maven plugins are designed to enhance the build process by automating common tasks and providing additional functionality. They allow developers to easily integrate various tools and technologies into their Maven projects without the need for manual configuration. Plugins are written in Java and can be executed within the Maven build lifecycle.

Plugins are defined in the project's POM (Project Object Model) file, which serves as the configuration file for Maven. Each plugin is associated with a specific goal, which represents a specific task that the plugin can perform. Goals can be executed individually or as part of a larger build process.

Using Built-in Maven Plugins

Apache Maven comes with a wide range of built-in plugins that cover common development tasks. These plugins are maintained by the Apache Maven community and are readily available for use in your projects. Some of the most commonly used built-in plugins include the Compiler Plugin, Surefire Plugin, and Jar Plugin.

To use a built-in plugin, you need to add its configuration to the *<plugins>* section of your project's POM file. The configuration includes the plugin's group ID, artifact ID, and version, as well as any additional parameters required for the plugin to function correctly. Once the plugin is configured, you can execute its goals by running the corresponding Maven command.

Creating Custom Maven Plugins

While the built-in plugins cover many common use cases, there may be situations where you need to create a custom plugin to meet specific project requirements. Maven provides a framework for developing custom plugins, allowing you to extend the functionality of the build system to suit your needs.

To create a custom Maven plugin, you need to define a Maven plugin project using a specific directory structure and Maven archetype. The plugin project should include a Java class that implements the desired functionality and a POM file that defines the plugin's configuration.

Once the plugin project is set up, you can build and install the plugin to your local Maven repository using the *mvn install* command. After installation, the plugin can be used in other Maven projects by adding its configuration to the POM file, just like with built-in plugins.

Configuring Maven Plugins

Maven plugins can be configured using the *<configuration>* element within the plugin's configuration block in the POM file. The configuration element allows you to specify various parameters and options that control the behavior of the plugin.

The specific configuration options available for a plugin depend on the plugin itself and its goals. The plugin's documentation should provide details on the available configuration options and their usage. It is important to carefully review the documentation to ensure that the plugin is configured correctly and that the desired behavior is achieved.

Executing Maven Plugins

Maven plugins are executed as part of the build process, either automatically or by explicitly invoking their goals. When a plugin is executed, it performs the tasks associated with its goals, such as compiling code, running tests, or generating reports.

To execute a plugin's goal, you can use the *mvn <plugin-prefix>:<goal>* command, where *<plugin-prefix>* is the prefix associated with the plugin and *<goal>* is the specific goal to execute. For example, to compile the project's source code using the Compiler Plugin, you would run *mvn compiler:compile*.

Troubleshooting Maven Plugins

Sometimes, issues may arise when using Maven plugins, such as compatibility problems, configuration errors, or unexpected behavior. When troubleshooting plugin-related problems, it is important to follow a systematic approach to identify and resolve the issue.

First, check the plugin's documentation and the Maven project's documentation for any known issues or limitations. Make sure that the plugin version you are using is compatible with your project's dependencies and the version of Maven you are using.

If the issue persists, try to isolate the problem by creating a minimal, reproducible example. This can help identify any conflicting configurations or dependencies that may be causing the problem. Additionally, enabling debug or verbose output can provide more detailed information about the plugin's execution and help pinpoint the issue.

If all else fails, consider reaching out to the plugin's community or support channels for assistance. The Apache Maven community is active and responsive, and there are many resources available online where you can seek help and guidance.

In the next section, we will delve deeper into using built-in Maven plugins and explore some of the most commonly used ones in more detail.

3.2 Using Built-in Maven Plugins

Maven is a powerful build automation tool that provides a wide range of built-in plugins to help streamline the development process. These plugins offer various functionalities, such as compiling code, running tests, generating reports, and deploying artifacts. In this section, we will explore some of the most commonly used built-in Maven plugins and learn how to leverage their capabilities to enhance our projects.

3.2.1 Compiler Plugin

The Compiler Plugin is one of the essential plugins in Maven, as it is responsible for compiling the source code of our project. By default, Maven uses the Java Compiler Plugin, which supports different versions of the Java programming language. However, we can configure the plugin to use a specific version of the compiler or customize its behavior according to our project requirements.

To configure the Compiler Plugin, we need to add the *<build>* element to our project's POM (Project Object Model) file and specify the plugin configuration within the *<plugins>* section. We can define the source and target Java versions, enable or disable specific compiler options, and even configure the plugin to generate debug information or optimize the compiled code.

3.2.2 Surefire Plugin

The Surefire Plugin is used for executing unit tests within our Maven project. It automatically detects and runs all the tests located in the default test source directory (*src/test/java*) or any other specified directory. The plugin generates detailed test reports, including information about the test results, test coverage, and execution time.

To use the Surefire Plugin, we need to include it in the *<plugins>* section of our project's POM file. By default, the plugin follows the naming convention for test classes (**Test.java*), but we can customize this behavior if needed. Additionally, we can configure various options, such as excluding specific tests, defining test suites, or specifying the test execution order.

3.2.3 Jar Plugin

The Jar Plugin is responsible for creating a JAR (Java Archive) file from our project's compiled classes and resources. This plugin is particularly useful when we want to package our project as a standalone executable or library that can be easily distributed and used by other projects.

To use the Jar Plugin, we need to add it to the *<plugins>* section of our POM file. By default, the plugin includes all the compiled classes and resources in the JAR file. However, we can customize the plugin configuration to exclude specific files or directories, include additional files, or even specify a custom manifest file.

3.2.4 Surefire Report Plugin

The Surefire Report Plugin generates detailed HTML reports based on the test results produced by the Surefire Plugin. These reports provide valuable insights into the test coverage, failures, and errors, helping us identify and fix issues in our codebase.

To generate the Surefire reports, we need to include the Surefire Report Plugin in the *<reporting>* section of our POM file. Once configured, Maven will automatically generate the reports during the build process. The generated reports can be accessed in the *target/site/surefire-report.html* directory of our project.

3.2.5 Javadoc Plugin

The Javadoc Plugin is used to generate API documentation from our project's source code. It automatically extracts the comments and annotations from the code and generates HTML pages that describe the classes, interfaces, methods, and fields.

To generate the Javadoc documentation, we need to include the Javadoc Plugin in the *<plugins>* section of our POM file. By default, the plugin generates the documentation in the *target/site/apidocs* directory. We can also customize the plugin configuration to include or exclude specific packages, classes, or members from the generated documentation.

3.2.6 Dependency Plugin

The Dependency Plugin provides various goals to analyze and manage dependencies within our Maven project. It allows us to list all the dependencies used by our project, analyze their versions, and even generate reports to visualize the dependency tree.

To use the Dependency Plugin, we need to include it in the *<plugins>* section of our POM file. We can then execute different goals, such as *dependency:tree* to display the dependency tree, *dependency:list* to list all the project dependencies, or *dependency:analyze* to identify potential issues with our dependencies, such as unused or conflicting versions.

3.2.7 Clean Plugin

The Clean Plugin is used to remove the generated build artifacts and clean the project directory. It is particularly useful when we want to start a fresh build or when we need to ensure that all the previous build artifacts are removed before starting a new build.

To use the Clean Plugin, we need to include it in the *<plugins>* section of our POM file. By default, the plugin removes the *target* directory, which contains the compiled classes, generated JAR files, and other build artifacts. However, we can customize the plugin configuration to include or exclude additional directories or files from the cleaning process.

These are just a few examples of the built-in Maven plugins available to us. Maven provides a vast collection of plugins that cater to various development needs. By leveraging these plugins, we can automate repetitive tasks, improve code quality, generate reports, and simplify the overall build and deployment process of our projects.

3.3 Creating Custom Maven Plugins

In addition to the built-in plugins provided by Apache Maven, developers also have the ability to create their own custom Maven plugins. This allows for greater flexibility and customization in the build process, as developers can define specific tasks and goals that are tailored to their project's requirements.

Creating a custom Maven plugin involves writing Java code that extends the *AbstractMojo* class provided by the Maven Plugin API. This class provides a set of methods and annotations that allow developers to define the behavior of their plugin. The *AbstractMojo* class also handles the configuration and execution of the plugin.

3.3.1 Setting up the Maven Plugin Project

To create a custom Maven plugin, the first step is to set up a Maven project specifically for the plugin. This project will contain the necessary dependencies and configurations for building and packaging the plugin.

To create the plugin project, follow these steps:

1. Open a command prompt or terminal and navigate to the directory where you want to create the project.

2. Run the following command to create a new Maven project:

```
mvn archetype:generate -DgroupId=com.example -DartifactId=my-plugin -DarchetypeArtifactId=maven-archetype-quickstart -DinteractiveMode=false
```

   This command creates a new Maven project using the *maven-archetype-quickstart* archetype, which provides a basic project structure for a Java application.

3. Navigate into the newly created project directory:

```
cd my-plugin
```

4. Open the *pom.xml* file in a text editor and add the necessary configurations for the plugin. This includes specifying the *groupId, artifactId,* and *version* of the plugin, as well as any dependencies required for the plugin's functionality.

3.3.2 Implementing the Custom Maven Plugin

Once the Maven plugin project is set up, the next step is to implement the functionality of the plugin. This involves creating a Java class that extends the *AbstractMojo* class and overriding the necessary methods.

To implement the custom Maven plugin, follow these steps:

1. Create a new Java class in the *src/main/java* directory of the plugin project. This class should extend the *AbstractMojo* class and implement the necessary methods.

2. Override the *execute()* method, which is the entry point for the plugin's execution. This method will contain the logic for the plugin's functionality.

3. Use the available methods and annotations provided by the *AbstractMojo* class to define the plugin's behavior. For example, the *@Parameter* annotation can be used to define configuration parameters for the plugin, and the *getLog()* method can be used to log messages during the plugin's execution.

4. Implement the desired functionality of the plugin within the *execute()* method. This can include tasks such as generating code, running tests, or deploying artifacts.

3.3.3 Building and Packaging the Custom Maven Plugin

Once the custom Maven plugin is implemented, it needs to be built and packaged so that it can be used in other Maven projects.

To build and package the custom Maven plugin, follow these steps:

1. Open a command prompt or terminal and navigate to the root directory of the plugin project.
2. Run the following command to build the plugin:

```
mvn clean install
```

   This command compiles the plugin's source code, runs any tests, and packages the plugin into a JAR file.

3. After the build is successful, the plugin JAR file will be located in the `target` directory of the plugin project.

3.3.4 Using the Custom Maven Plugin

Once the custom Maven plugin is built and packaged, it can be used in other Maven projects by adding it as a dependency in the project's `pom.xml` file.

To use the custom Maven plugin, follow these steps:

1. Open the `pom.xml` file of the project where you want to use the custom plugin.
2. Add the following `<plugin>` configuration to the `<build>` section of the `pom.xml` file:

```
<build>
  <plugins>
    <plugin>
      <groupId>com.example</groupId>
      <artifactId>my-plugin</artifactId>
      <version>1.0.0</version>
    </plugin>
  </plugins>
</build>
```

Replace `com.example` with the `groupId` of the custom plugin, and `my-plugin` with the `artifactId` of the custom plugin.

3. Save the `pom.xml` file.

4. Run the desired Maven command to execute the custom plugin. For example, if the custom plugin defines a goal called `my-goal`, you can run the following command:

```
mvn my-plugin:my-goal
```

This command will execute the custom plugin and perform the defined tasks and goals.

By creating custom Maven plugins, developers can extend the functionality of Apache Maven and tailor the build process to their specific project requirements. This allows for greater flexibility and control over the build and deployment process, ultimately leading to more efficient and streamlined development workflows.

3.4 Configuring Maven Plugins

Maven plugins are an essential part of the Maven build process. They provide additional functionality and can be used to customize and extend the build lifecycle. In this section, we will explore how to configure Maven plugins to suit your project's specific requirements.

3.4.1 Plugin Configuration in the POM

Maven plugins are configured in the project's POM (Project Object Model) file. The POM is an XML file that contains information about the project and its configuration. To configure a plugin, you need to add a plugin section within the build section of the POM.

Here is an example of how a plugin section is structured in the POM:

```
<build>
  <plugins>
    <plugin>
      <groupId>...</groupId>
      <artifactId>...</artifactId>
      <version>...</version>
      <configuration>
        <!-- Plugin configuration parameters -->
      </configuration>
    </plugin>
  </plugins>
</build>
```

In the plugin section, you need to specify the plugin's *groupId*, *artifactId*, and *version*. These values uniquely identify the plugin and determine which version of the plugin will be used in the build process.

The *configuration* element is where you can specify the plugin's configuration parameters. These parameters vary depending on the plugin and the functionality it provides. You can refer to the plugin's documentation to understand the available configuration options.

3.4.2 Plugin Goals and Phases

Maven plugins are executed during specific phases of the build lifecycle. Each plugin can define one or more goals, which represent specific tasks that the plugin can perform. Goals are bound to specific phases of the build lifecycle, and they are executed when the corresponding phase is reached.

For example, the *compile* phase is responsible for compiling the project's source code. The *maven-compiler-plugin* is a built-in Maven plugin that provides the *compile* goal, which is bound to the *compile* phase. When the *compile* phase is reached during the build process, the *compile* goal of the *maven-compiler-plugin* is executed.

To configure a plugin goal, you need to specify the goal name within the plugin's configuration section in the POM. Here is an example:

```
<build>
  <plugins>
    <plugin>
      <groupId>org.apache.maven.plugins</groupId>
      <artifactId>maven-compiler-plugin</artifactId>
      <version>3.8.1</version>
      <configuration>
        <source>1.8</source>
        <target>1.8</target>
      </configuration>
    </plugin>
  </plugins>
</build>
```

In this example, the *maven-compiler-plugin* is configured with the *source* and *target* parameters set to *1.8*. This specifies that the source code should be compiled to be compatible with Java 1.8.

3.4.3 Plugin Dependencies

Plugins can have dependencies on other plugins or libraries. These dependencies are specified within the plugin's configuration section in the POM. Maven will automatically resolve and download the required dependencies before executing the plugin.

To specify plugin dependencies, you need to add a *dependencies* element within the plugin's configuration section. Here is an example:

```
<build>
  <plugins>
    <plugin>
      <groupId>org.apache.maven.plugins</groupId>
      <artifactId>maven-compiler-plugin</artifactId>
      <version>3.8.1</version>
      <configuration>
        <!-- Plugin configuration parameters -->
      </configuration>
      <dependencies>
        <dependency>
          <groupId>com.example</groupId>
          <artifactId>my-library</artifactId>
          <version>1.0.0</version>
        </dependency>
      </dependencies>
    </plugin>
  </plugins>
</build>
```

In this example, the *maven-compiler-plugin* has a dependency on the *my-library* artifact with version *1.0.0* from the *com.example* group. Maven will resolve and download this dependency before executing the plugin.

3.4.4 Plugin Execution Order

The order in which plugins are executed can be important, especially when plugins have dependencies on each other. Maven follows a specific order when executing plugins during the build process.

By default, plugins are executed in the order they are defined in the POM. However, you can explicitly specify the execution order using the *executions* element within the plugin's configuration section. The *executions* element allows you to define multiple executions of a plugin, each with its own configuration and phase.

Here is an example of how to define multiple executions for a plugin:

```
<build>
  <plugins>
    <plugin>
      <groupId>org.apache.maven.plugins</groupId>
      <artifactId>maven-compiler-plugin</artifactId>
      <version>3.8.1</version>
      <executions>
        <execution>
          <id>first-execution</id>
          <phase>compile</phase>
          <goals>
            <goal>compile</goal>
          </goals>
          <configuration>
            <!-- Configuration for the first execution -->
          </configuration>
        </execution>
        <execution>
          <id>second-execution</id>
          <phase>test</phase>
          <goals>
            <goal>testCompile</goal>
          </goals>
          <configuration>
            <!-- Configuration for the second execution -->
          </configuration>
        </execution>
      </executions>
    </plugin>
  </plugins>
</build>
```

In this example, the *maven-compiler-plugin* is configured with two executions. The first execution is bound to the *compile* phase and executes the *compile* goal. The second execution is bound to the *test* phase and executes the *testCompile* goal.

By explicitly defining the execution order, you can ensure that plugins are executed in the desired sequence and that any dependencies between plugins are properly resolved.

3.4.5 Plugin Configuration Inheritance

Maven supports inheritance of plugin configurations from parent POMs. This means that if a plugin is configured in a parent POM, its configuration will be inherited by child projects unless overridden.

To inherit a plugin configuration, you need to define the plugin in the parent POM's build section without specifying the configuration. Then, in the child project's POM, you can override the inherited configuration by redefining the plugin with its own configuration.

This allows you to define common plugin configurations in a parent POM and have them automatically applied to all child projects. It promotes consistency and reduces duplication of configuration across multiple projects.

Conclusion

Configuring Maven plugins is an important aspect of building projects with Apache Maven. By understanding how to configure plugins in the POM, specify plugin goals and phases, manage plugin dependencies, control plugin execution order, and leverage plugin configuration inheritance, you can effectively customize and extend the Maven build process to meet your project's specific requirements.

3.5 Executing Maven Plugins

Maven plugins are an essential part of the Maven build process. They provide additional functionality and can be used to perform various tasks such as compiling code, running tests, generating reports, and deploying artifacts. In this section, we will explore how to execute Maven plugins and leverage their capabilities to enhance your build process.

3.5.1 Plugin Execution

Maven plugins are executed during different phases of the build lifecycle. Each plugin is bound to one or more lifecycle phases, and when that phase is reached, the plugin is automatically executed. The execution of plugins can be configured in the project's POM (Project Object Model) file.

To execute a plugin, you need to specify its groupId, artifactId, and version in the POM file. Additionally, you can configure the plugin's goals, which are the specific tasks that the plugin will perform. The goals can be executed individually or as part of a plugin's default execution.

Here is an example of how to configure the execution of a plugin in the POM file:

```
<build>
  <plugins>
    <plugin>
      <groupId>com.example</groupId>
      <artifactId>my-plugin</artifactId>
      <version>1.0.0</version>
      <executions>
        <execution>
          <id>my-execution</id>
          <phase>compile</phase>
          <goals>
            <goal>my-goal</goal>
          </goals>
        </execution>
      </executions>
    </plugin>
  </plugins>
</build>
```

In this example, the plugin with groupId “com.example” and artifactId “my-plugin” will be executed during the “compile” phase of the build lifecycle. The plugin’s goal “my-goal” will be executed as part of the default execution.

3.5.2 Plugin Configuration

Plugins can be further configured to customize their behavior. Configuration parameters can be specified within the plugin’s configuration section in the POM file. These parameters vary depending on the plugin and its goals.

Here is an example of how to configure a plugin in the POM file:

```
<build>
  <plugins>
    <plugin>
      <groupId>com.example</groupId>
      <artifactId>my-plugin</artifactId>
      <version>1.0.0</version>
      <executions>
        <execution>
          <id>my-execution</id>
          <phase>compile</phase>
          <goals>
            <goal>my-goal</goal>
          </goals>
          <configuration>
            <param1>value1</param1>
            <param2>value2</param2>
          </configuration>
        </execution>
      </executions>
    </plugin>
  </plugins>
</build>
```

In this example, the plugin's configuration section contains two parameters: "param1" and "param2" with their respective values. These parameters will be passed to the plugin during execution and can be used to customize its behavior.

3.5.3 Plugin Dependency Resolution

Plugins can have dependencies on other libraries or plugins. Maven automatically resolves these dependencies and ensures that they are available during plugin execution. The plugin's dependencies can be specified in the POM file, similar to regular project dependencies.

Here is an example of how to specify plugin dependencies in the POM file:

```
<build>
  <plugins>
    <plugin>
      <groupId>com.example</groupId>
      <artifactId>my-plugin</artifactId>
      <version>1.0.0</version>
      <dependencies>
        <dependency>
          <groupId>com.example</groupId>
          <artifactId>my-library</artifactId>
          <version>1.0.0</version>
        </dependency>
      </dependencies>
    </plugin>
  </plugins>
</build>
```

In this example, the plugin has a dependency on the library with groupId "com.example" and artifactId "my-library" version 1.0.0. Maven will automatically resolve and include this dependency when executing the plugin.

3.5.4 Plugin Execution Order

The order in which plugins are executed can be important, especially when multiple plugins are bound to the same phase. By default, plugins are executed in the order they are defined in the POM file. However, you can explicitly specify the execution order using the `<executions>` section.

Here is an example of how to specify the execution order of plugins in the POM file:

```
<build>
  <plugins>
    <plugin>
      <groupId>com.example</groupId>
      <artifactId>plugin1</artifactId>
      <version>1.0.0</version>
      <executions>
        <execution>
          <id>execution1</id>
          <phase>compile</phase>
          <goals>
            <goal>goal1</goal>
          </goals>
        </execution>
      </executions>
    </plugin>
    <plugin>
      <groupId>com.example</groupId>
      <artifactId>plugin2</artifactId>
      <version>1.0.0</version>
      <executions>
        <execution>
          <id>execution2</id>
          <phase>compile</phase>
          <goals>
            <goal>goal2</goal>
          </goals>
        </execution>
      </executions>
    </plugin>
  </plugins>
</build>
```

In this example, “plugin1” will be executed before “plugin2” during the “compile” phase because it is defined first in the POM file. If the order needs to be reversed, you can simply swap the positions of the plugins.

3.5.5 Skipping Plugin Execution

Sometimes, you may want to skip the execution of a plugin for a specific build. Maven provides a mechanism to skip plugin execution using the *-Dmaven.test.skip=true* command-line option. This option can be used to skip the execution of all plugins during the build.

Alternatively, you can skip the execution of a specific plugin by configuring the *<skip>* parameter in the plugin's configuration section.

Here is an example of how to skip the execution of a plugin in the POM file:

```
<build>
  <plugins>
    <plugin>
      <groupId>com.example</groupId>
      <artifactId>my-plugin</artifactId>
      <version>1.0.0</version>
      <executions>
        <execution>
          <id>my-execution</id>
          <phase>compile</phase>
          <goals>
            <goal>my-goal</goal>
          </goals>
          <configuration>
            <skip>true</skip>
          </configuration>
        </execution>
      </executions>
    </plugin>
  </plugins>
</build>
```

In this example, the execution of the plugin "my-plugin" will be skipped during the "compile" phase.

3.5.6 Summary

In this section, we have learned how to execute Maven plugins and configure their behavior. We explored the plugin execution order, skipping plugin execution, and specifying plugin dependencies. Understanding how to effectively use plugins is crucial for enhancing your build process and automating various tasks in your project.

3.6 Troubleshooting Maven Plugins

Maven plugins are an essential part of the Maven build process, providing additional functionality and extending the capabilities of Maven. However, like any software, plugins can sometimes encounter issues or errors that need to be resolved. In this section, we will explore common troubleshooting techniques for Maven plugins.

3.6.1 Plugin Version Compatibility

One common issue when working with Maven plugins is version compatibility. Maven plugins are regularly updated to fix bugs, introduce new features, or improve performance. However, using an incompatible version of a plugin can lead to unexpected behavior or errors.

To troubleshoot version compatibility issues, it is important to ensure that the plugin version specified in the project's POM (Project Object Model) is compatible with the version of Maven being used. Maven plugins often have specific requirements for the minimum version of Maven they can work with.

To check the compatibility of a plugin version with your Maven installation, you can refer to the plugin's documentation or the Maven Central Repository. The documentation usually provides information about the supported Maven versions and any known compatibility issues.

If you encounter compatibility issues, you can try updating the plugin version in your POM to a compatible version. Alternatively, you can consider downgrading your Maven version to match the plugin's requirements.

3.6.2 Plugin Configuration Errors

Another common source of issues with Maven plugins is incorrect or incomplete configuration. Maven plugins rely on configuration parameters to perform their tasks correctly. If the configuration is not set up properly, the plugin may fail or produce unexpected results.

To troubleshoot plugin configuration errors, it is important to carefully review the plugin's documentation and ensure that all required configuration parameters are correctly specified in the POM. Pay attention to the syntax and formatting requirements specified by the plugin.

If you are still encountering issues, you can try validating your POM using the Maven command-line tool. The *mvn validate* command can help identify any syntax errors or missing configuration elements in your POM.

Additionally, some plugins provide verbose output or debug options that can help diagnose configuration issues. You can enable these options by adding the appropriate configuration parameters to your POM or by using command-line options when executing Maven.

3.6.3 Plugin Dependency Issues

Maven plugins often rely on other plugins or external libraries to function correctly. If these dependencies are not resolved properly, it can lead to plugin failures or errors.

To troubleshoot plugin dependency issues, you can start by checking the plugin's documentation for any specific dependency requirements. Ensure that all required dependencies are correctly specified in the POM and that their versions are compatible with the plugin.

If you are still experiencing dependency issues, you can use the Maven dependency plugin to analyze the plugin's dependencies and their resolution. The *mvn dependency:tree* command can provide a tree-like representation of the plugin's dependencies, allowing you to identify any conflicts or missing dependencies.

In some cases, conflicts may arise when multiple plugins require different versions of the same dependency. Maven provides mechanisms like dependency management and exclusions to resolve such conflicts. You can use these mechanisms to align the versions of conflicting dependencies or exclude unnecessary dependencies.

3.6.4 Plugin Execution Order

Maven plugins are executed in a specific order defined by the Maven build lifecycle. However, there may be cases where the execution order of plugins needs to be modified or adjusted.

To troubleshoot plugin execution order issues, you can review the plugin's documentation to understand its intended execution phase. Ensure that the plugin is bound to the correct phase in the POM.

If you need to modify the execution order of plugins, you can use the `<executions>` element in the plugin configuration. This allows you to specify multiple executions of the same plugin or control the order in which plugins are executed within a phase.

3.6.5 Plugin Output and Logging

When troubleshooting Maven plugins, it is important to examine the plugin's output and logging information. Plugins often provide valuable information about their execution, including error messages, warnings, or debug output.

To capture and analyze the plugin's output, you can redirect the Maven build output to a file using the `-l` or `--log-file` option. This allows you to review the output in detail and identify any error messages or warnings.

Additionally, some plugins provide logging options that can be enabled to obtain more detailed information about their execution. These options can help diagnose issues by providing insights into the plugin's internal processes and interactions with other components.

3.6.6 Community Support and Issue Tracking

If you have exhausted all troubleshooting options and are still unable to resolve the issue with a Maven plugin, it can be helpful to seek assistance from the community. Maven has a large and active user community, and there are several resources available for support.

You can start by searching online forums, mailing lists, or Stack Overflow for similar issues or questions related to the plugin you are troubleshooting. Often, someone else may have encountered a similar problem and found a solution.

If you are unable to find a solution, you can consider posting a question on a relevant forum or mailing list, providing detailed information about the issue, including the plugin version, Maven version, and any error messages or logs. The community members are usually helpful and willing to assist in troubleshooting.

Additionally, many Maven plugins have their own issue tracking systems, where you can report bugs or request assistance. These systems allow you to provide detailed information about the issue and track its progress towards resolution.

In conclusion, troubleshooting Maven plugins involves understanding version compatibility, reviewing and correcting plugin configuration, resolving dependency issues, managing plugin execution order, analyzing plugin output and logging, and seeking community support when needed. By following these troubleshooting techniques, you can effectively resolve issues and ensure the smooth execution of Maven plugins in your projects.

4 Managing Dependencies with Maven

4.1 Understanding Dependency Management in Maven

Dependency management is a crucial aspect of any software development project. It involves managing the external libraries and frameworks that your project relies on. Apache Maven provides a powerful and efficient way to handle dependencies in your project.

4.1.1 What are Dependencies?

Dependencies are external libraries or frameworks that your project needs in order to compile, build, and run successfully. These dependencies can include Java libraries, third-party frameworks, or even other modules within your project. Managing dependencies manually can be a tedious and error-prone task, especially when dealing with complex projects with multiple dependencies.

4.1.2 Why is Dependency Management Important?

Dependency management plays a vital role in ensuring that your project is built and executed correctly. Here are a few reasons why it is important:

1. **Simplifies Project Setup**: With dependency management, you don't have to manually download and configure each library or framework your project requires. Maven takes care of resolving and downloading the necessary dependencies automatically.

2. **Ensures Consistency**: Dependency management ensures that all developers working on the project are using the same versions of libraries and frameworks. This helps avoid conflicts and compatibility issues.

3. **Saves Time and Effort**: Maven handles the tedious task of resolving and downloading dependencies, saving

developers time and effort. It also simplifies the process of updating dependencies to newer versions.

4. **Facilitates Collaboration**: When working on a team project, dependency management allows all team members to easily share and synchronize the project's dependencies. This promotes collaboration and reduces the chances of errors.

4.1.3 How Does Maven Handle Dependency Management?

Maven uses a declarative approach to manage dependencies. It relies on a project object model (POM) file, which is an XML file that describes the project's configuration, including its dependencies. The POM file acts as a central source of information for Maven to resolve and download the required dependencies.

When Maven builds a project, it reads the POM file and retrieves the necessary dependencies from a remote repository or a local cache. It then adds these dependencies to the project's classpath, allowing the project to compile and run successfully.

4.1.4 Declaring Dependencies in the POM

To declare dependencies in your project's POM file, you need to specify the group ID, artifact ID, and version of each dependency. The group ID represents the organization or group that created the dependency, the artifact ID is the name of the dependency, and the version indicates the specific version of the dependency you want to use.

Maven uses a coordinated versioning system, which allows you to specify a range of versions for a dependency. For example, you can declare a dependency with a version range of `[1.0,2.0)`, which means any version from `1.0` (inclusive) to `2.0` (exclusive) is acceptable.

4.1.5 Resolving Dependencies

Once you have declared the dependencies in your POM file, Maven takes care of resolving them. It searches for the dependencies in the following order:

1. **Local Repository**: Maven first checks if the required dependencies are already present in the local repository on your machine. If found, it uses the local copy instead of downloading it again.

2. **Remote Repository**: If the dependencies are not available in the local repository, Maven searches for them in the remote repositories specified in the POM file. These remote repositories can be public repositories like Maven Central or private repositories hosted within your organization.

3. **Transitive Dependencies**: Maven also resolves transitive dependencies, which are dependencies required by your project's direct dependencies. For example, if your project depends on library A, which in turn depends on library B, Maven will automatically resolve and download both A and B.

4.1.6 Managing Transitive Dependencies

Transitive dependencies can sometimes lead to conflicts or compatibility issues. Maven provides mechanisms to manage transitive dependencies effectively:

1. **Dependency Exclusion**: You can exclude specific transitive dependencies by declaring exclusions in your POM file. This allows you to control which dependencies are included in your project and avoid conflicts.

2. **Dependency Management**: Maven allows you to define a dependency management section in your POM file. In this section, you can specify the versions of dependencies

used by your project, including transitive dependencies. This ensures consistency and avoids conflicts caused by different versions of the same dependency.

3. **Dependency Scope**: Maven provides different dependency scopes, such as compile, test, runtime, and provided. Scopes define the visibility and availability of dependencies during different phases of the build process. Choosing the appropriate scope for each dependency helps manage their usage and reduces the chances of conflicts.

In conclusion, understanding dependency management in Maven is essential for efficient and reliable software development. Maven simplifies the process of handling dependencies, ensuring consistency, saving time, and facilitating collaboration. By declaring dependencies in the POM file and leveraging Maven's dependency resolution mechanism, you can effectively manage dependencies and avoid conflicts in your projects.

4.2 Declaring Dependencies in the POM

In Apache Maven, dependencies are an essential aspect of managing a project's external libraries and frameworks. Maven provides a straightforward and efficient way to declare and manage dependencies through the Project Object Model (POM). The POM is an XML file that serves as the backbone of a Maven project, containing information about the project and its dependencies.

4.2.1 Understanding Dependency Declarations

To declare a dependency in the POM, you need to specify the group ID, artifact ID, and version of the dependency. The group ID represents the organization or group that created the dependency, while the artifact ID is the unique identifier for the dependency itself. The version number indicates the specific version of the dependency that your project requires.

Here's an example of a dependency declaration in the POM:

```
<dependencies>
    <dependency>
        <groupId>com.example</groupId>
        <artifactId>my-library</artifactId>
        <version>1.0.0</version>
    </dependency>
</dependencies>
```

In this example, the project depends on a library with the group ID "com.example," artifact ID "my-library," and version "1.0.0." Maven uses this information to resolve and download the required dependency from the configured repositories.

4.2.2 Specifying Dependency Scope

In addition to the basic dependency declaration, Maven allows you to specify the scope of a dependency. The scope determines how the dependency is used during different phases of the build process. Maven provides several predefined scopes, including:

- **compile**: This is the default scope and indicates that the dependency is required for compilation and runtime.
- **provided**: Dependencies with this scope are required for compilation but are expected to be provided by the runtime environment.
- **runtime**: Dependencies with this scope are required for runtime but not for compilation.
- **test**: Dependencies with this scope are only required for testing purposes and are not included in the runtime classpath.

To specify the scope of a dependency, you can add the *<scope>* element within the *<dependency>* block:

```
<dependencies>
    <dependency>
        <groupId>com.example</groupId>
        <artifactId>my-library</artifactId>
        <version>1.0.0</version>
        <scope>compile</scope>
    </dependency>
</dependencies>
```

In this example, the dependency has a scope of "compile," indicating that it is required for both compilation and runtime.

4.2.3 Managing Dependency Exclusions

Sometimes, a dependency may bring along its own set of transitive dependencies that conflict with other dependencies in your project. In such cases, you can exclude specific transitive dependencies to avoid conflicts and ensure the correct versions are used.

To exclude a transitive dependency, you can add an *<exclusions>* block within the *<dependency>* block and specify the group ID and artifact ID of the dependency to be excluded:

```
<dependencies>
    <dependency>
        <groupId>com.example</groupId>
        <artifactId>my-library</artifactId>
        <version>1.0.0</version>
        <exclusions>
            <exclusion>
                <groupId>org.conflicting</groupId>
                <artifactId>conflicting-library</artifactId
>
            </exclusion>
        </exclusions>
    </dependency>
</dependencies>
```

In this example, the transitive dependency with the group ID "org.conflicting" and artifact ID "conflicting-library" will be excluded when resolving dependencies.

4.2.4 Dependency Management

Maven also provides a powerful feature called "Dependency Management" that allows you to centralize and control the versions of dependencies used across multiple projects. By declaring a dependency in the *<dependencyManagement>* section of the POM, you can specify the version to be used by all projects within the current project hierarchy.

Here's an example of how to use the *<dependencyManagement>* section:

```
<dependencyManagement>
    <dependencies>
        <dependency>
            <groupId>com.example</groupId>
            <artifactId>my-library</artifactId>
            <version>1.0.0</version>
        </dependency>
    </dependencies>
</dependencyManagement>
```

By declaring the dependency in the *<dependencyManagement>* section, you can omit the version declaration in the individual project's *<dependencies>* section. Maven will automatically use the version specified in the *<dependencyManagement>* section.

4.2.5 Importing Dependencies from Other POMs

In large projects or multi-module projects, it is common to have multiple POM files. In such cases, you can import dependencies from other POM files using the *<dependencyManagement>* section.

To import dependencies from another POM, you need to add the *<dependencyManagement>* section within the importing POM and specify the *<groupId>*, *<artifactId>*, and *<version>* of the POM to be imported:

```
<dependencyManagement>
    <dependencies>
        <dependency>
            <groupId>com.example</groupId>
            <artifactId>my-library</artifactId>
            <version>1.0.0</version>
            <type>pom</type>
            <scope>import</scope>
        </dependency>
    </dependencies>
</dependencyManagement>
```

In this example, the POM with the group ID "com.example," artifact ID "my-library," and version "1.0.0" will be imported, and its dependencies will be available for use in the importing POM.

4.2.6 Dependency Ordering

Maven automatically resolves and downloads dependencies based on their declared order in the POM file. If a dependency has multiple versions declared in different parts of the POM hierarchy, Maven uses the nearest declaration to resolve the version conflict.

It is important to ensure that the order of dependencies in the POM reflects the correct dependency hierarchy. If the order is incorrect, it may lead to unexpected behavior or conflicts during the build process.

Conclusion

Declaring dependencies in the POM is a fundamental aspect of managing dependencies in Apache Maven. By understanding how to declare dependencies, specify their scope, manage exclusions, and utilize dependency management, you can effectively manage and control the external libraries and frameworks used in your Maven projects.

4.3 Resolving Dependencies

In Apache Maven, resolving dependencies is a crucial aspect of building projects. Maven uses a powerful dependency management system that simplifies the process of including external libraries and frameworks in your project. This section will explore how Maven resolves dependencies and ensures that all required dependencies are available during the build process.

4.3.1 Dependency Resolution Process

When Maven builds a project, it follows a specific process to resolve dependencies. This process involves the following steps:

1. **Dependency Declaration**: In the project's POM file, you declare the dependencies that your project requires. These declarations include the artifact coordinates, such as the group ID, artifact ID, and version.

2. **Dependency Collection**: Maven collects all the declared dependencies and creates a dependency tree. This tree represents the hierarchical structure of the project's dependencies, including transitive dependencies.

3. **Dependency Resolution**: Maven starts resolving the dependencies by searching for them in the local repository. The local repository is a local cache where Maven stores all the downloaded dependencies. If the dependencies are not found in the local repository, Maven proceeds to the next step.

4. **Remote Repository Lookup**: Maven searches for the dependencies in the remote repositories specified in the project's POM file. These repositories can be either public repositories like Maven Central or private repositories hosted on a server. Maven downloads the required dependencies from the remote repositories and stores them in the local repository for future use.

5. **Version Conflict Resolution**: In some cases, multiple dependencies may have conflicting versions. Maven uses a set of rules to resolve these conflicts and determine the appropriate version to use. The rules prioritize the nearest definition of a dependency and the version declared in the project's POM file.

6. **Dependency Download**: Once the dependencies are resolved, Maven downloads them from the remote repositories and stores them in the local repository. This ensures that the dependencies are available for future builds and can be easily shared across different projects.

4.3.2 Dependency Scopes

In Maven, dependencies can have different scopes that define their visibility and usage within the project. Understanding these scopes is essential for managing dependencies effectively. Maven provides the following dependency scopes:

- **Compile**: Dependencies with the compile scope are required for compiling and running the project. These dependencies are included in the classpath of the project and are available during both compile-time and runtime.

- **Provided**: Dependencies with the provided scope are required for compiling the project but are expected to be provided by the runtime environment. These dependencies are not included in the final artifact as they are assumed to be available in the target environment.

- **Runtime**: Dependencies with the runtime scope are required for running the project but are not needed during compilation. These dependencies are not included in the classpath during compilation but are available during runtime.

- **Test**: Dependencies with the test scope are only required for running tests. These dependencies are not included in the final artifact and are used exclusively for testing purposes.

- **System**: Dependencies with the system scope are similar to provided dependencies but require an explicit path to be specified. These dependencies are not available in any repository and must be manually provided by the developer.
- **Import**: Dependencies with the import scope are used only in Maven's dependency management. They are not included in the classpath and are not used during the build process.

By understanding and correctly specifying the appropriate scope for each dependency, you can ensure that your project has the necessary dependencies at the right stages of the build process.

4.3.3 Dependency Exclusions

In some cases, you may want to exclude specific transitive dependencies that are brought in by other dependencies. Maven allows you to exclude these unwanted dependencies using the *<exclusions>* element in the dependency declaration. By specifying the artifact coordinates of the dependency to be excluded, Maven will ensure that it is not included in the build.

Excluding dependencies can be useful when you encounter conflicts or compatibility issues between different versions of the same library. By excluding the conflicting dependency, you can ensure that your project uses the desired version without any conflicts.

4.3.4 Dependency Caching

To improve build performance, Maven caches the resolved dependencies in the local repository. Once a dependency is downloaded, it is stored in the local repository and reused in subsequent builds. This caching mechanism reduces the need to download dependencies repeatedly, especially when working on multiple projects with the same dependencies.

However, it's important to note that the cached dependencies may become outdated over time. To ensure that you have the latest versions of the dependencies, you can use the *mvn dependency:purge-local-repository* command to clear the local repository cache and force Maven to download the dependencies again.

4.3.5 Offline Mode

Maven also provides an offline mode that allows you to build projects without accessing remote repositories. This can be useful in situations where you have limited or no internet connectivity. By enabling offline mode, Maven will only use the dependencies available in the local repository and will not attempt to download any dependencies from remote repositories.

To enable offline mode, you can use the *-o* or *--offline* command-line option when running Maven commands. This ensures that Maven operates in offline mode and does not make any network requests.

4.3.6 Dependency Management Best Practices

To effectively manage dependencies in your Maven projects, consider the following best practices:

- Regularly update your dependencies to the latest stable versions to benefit from bug fixes, performance improvements, and new features.

- Use specific version numbers for your dependencies instead of relying on ranges or dynamic versions. This ensures that your builds are reproducible and avoids unexpected changes due to version updates.
- Avoid unnecessary dependencies to keep your project lean and reduce the risk of conflicts or compatibility issues.
- Use the appropriate dependency scope for each dependency to ensure that they are included or excluded as needed during the build process.
- Document your project's dependencies and their versions in the project's POM file to provide clear and concise information for other developers working on the project.

By following these best practices, you can effectively manage dependencies in your Maven projects and ensure smooth and reliable builds. Maven's dependency management system provides a robust and flexible solution for handling dependencies, making it easier to build and maintain complex projects.

4.4 Managing Transitive Dependencies

In Apache Maven, managing dependencies is a crucial aspect of building and managing projects. When a project depends on a library or module, it often requires other dependencies as well. These additional dependencies are known as transitive dependencies. Managing transitive dependencies effectively is essential to ensure that your project has all the required dependencies and that they are compatible with each other.

4.4.1 Understanding Transitive Dependencies

Transitive dependencies are dependencies that are not explicitly declared in your project's POM file but are required by the direct dependencies. Maven automatically resolves and includes these transitive dependencies in your project's classpath during the build process.

For example, suppose your project depends on Library A, and Library A depends on Library B. In this case, Library B is a transitive dependency of your project. Maven will automatically download and include both Library A and Library B in your project's classpath.

Transitive dependencies can quickly become complex, especially in large projects with multiple dependencies. Maven simplifies this process by managing the transitive dependencies for you, ensuring that all required dependencies are included and resolving any conflicts that may arise.

4.4.2 Resolving Transitive Dependencies

Maven uses a process called dependency resolution to manage transitive dependencies. When you build your project, Maven analyzes the dependencies declared in your POM file and retrieves the required dependencies from remote repositories or your local repository.

During the resolution process, Maven checks the transitive dependencies of each direct dependency and ensures that they are also included. Maven follows a depth-first search algorithm to resolve dependencies, starting from the direct dependencies and recursively resolving their transitive dependencies.

Maven resolves conflicts that may arise when multiple dependencies require different versions of the same library. It uses a set of rules called dependency mediation to determine which version to include in the project. By default, Maven selects the version that is closest to the root of the dependency tree. However, you can override this behavior by explicitly specifying the version in your POM file.

4.4.3 Excluding Transitive Dependencies

In some cases, you may want to exclude specific transitive dependencies from being included in your project. Maven provides a mechanism to exclude dependencies using the *<exclusions>* element in the dependency declaration.

To exclude a transitive dependency, you need to identify the dependency and specify it in the *<exclusions>* section of the direct dependency. You can specify the artifact coordinates of the dependency, including the group ID, artifact ID, and version.

```
<dependency>
    <groupId>com.example</groupId>
    <artifactId>my-project</artifactId>
    <version>1.0.0</version>
    <exclusions>
        <exclusion>
            <groupId>com.example</groupId>
            <artifactId>unwanted-dependency</artifactId>
        </exclusion>
    </exclusions>
</dependency>
```

In the above example, the unwanted-dependency is excluded from the my-project dependency.

Excluding transitive dependencies should be used with caution, as it may lead to runtime errors if the excluded dependency is required by other parts of your project.

4.4.4 Managing Dependency Scope

In addition to excluding transitive dependencies, Maven allows you to manage the scope of dependencies. The scope determines when and how the dependency is used during the build process.

Maven provides several predefined scopes for dependencies, including:

- **compile**: This is the default scope. Dependencies with this scope are required for compiling and running the project.
- **provided**: Dependencies with this scope are required for compiling the project but are expected to be provided by the runtime environment.
- **runtime**: Dependencies with this scope are required for running the project but not for compiling it.
- **test**: Dependencies with this scope are only required for testing the project and are not included in the runtime classpath.
- **system**: Dependencies with this scope are similar to provided scope but require an explicit path to be specified.

By specifying the appropriate scope for your dependencies, you can control their inclusion in different phases of the build process. This helps in reducing the size of the final artifact and ensuring that only the necessary dependencies are included.

4.4.5 Managing Dependency Conflicts

In some cases, conflicts may arise when multiple dependencies require different versions of the same library. Maven provides several strategies to manage these conflicts and ensure that the correct version is included in the project.

- **Dependency mediation**: Maven uses dependency mediation to select the version of a library when conflicts occur. By default, Maven selects the version that is closest to the root of the dependency tree. However, you can override this behavior by explicitly specifying the version in your POM file.
- **Dependency management**: Maven allows you to define a dependency management section in your POM file. In this section, you can specify the versions of the dependencies used in your project. This ensures that all modules in your project use the same version of a library, resolving any conflicts.
- **Forced version**: If you encounter a conflict and want to force a specific version of a library, you can use the `<dependencyManagement>` section in your POM file. By specifying the desired version, Maven will use it regardless of any conflicting versions.

Managing dependency conflicts is crucial to ensure the stability and compatibility of your project. By understanding the different conflict resolution strategies provided by Maven, you can effectively manage and resolve any conflicts that may arise.

In this section, we discussed the concept of transitive dependencies in Apache Maven. We explored how Maven resolves and includes these dependencies in your project. We also learned how to exclude transitive dependencies, manage dependency scope, and handle dependency conflicts. By effectively managing transitive dependencies, you can ensure that your project has all the required dependencies and that they are compatible with each other.

5 Working with Maven Repositories

5.1 Introduction to Maven Repositories

In Apache Maven, repositories play a crucial role in managing dependencies and storing artifacts. A repository is a location where Maven can find and retrieve dependencies and plugins required for building a project. It acts as a centralized storage for all the artifacts that are used in the development process.

5.1.1 Local Repository

When you first install Maven, it automatically creates a local repository on your machine. This local repository is located in the *.m2* directory in your user's home directory. The local repository is used to store all the artifacts that are downloaded from remote repositories or installed locally.

The local repository acts as a cache for dependencies and plugins, so that Maven doesn't have to download them every time you build a project. It also allows you to work offline, as all the required artifacts are already available in the local repository.

5.1.2 Remote Repositories

Apart from the local repository, Maven also supports remote repositories. Remote repositories are external repositories that are hosted on remote servers and can be accessed over the internet. These repositories contain a vast collection of artifacts that can be used in your projects.

Maven uses the concept of "dependency resolution" to retrieve artifacts from remote repositories. When you specify a dependency in your project's POM (Project Object Model) file, Maven searches for that dependency in the local repository first. If it is not found, Maven then looks for the dependency in the remote repositories specified in the POM.

By default, Maven is configured to use the Maven Central Repository as the primary remote repository. The Maven Central Repository is a public repository that hosts a wide range of open-source artifacts. However, you can also configure Maven to use other remote repositories, such as private repositories or third-party repositories.

5.1.3 Repository Structure

Maven repositories follow a specific structure to organize and store artifacts. The structure consists of two main types of repositories: release repositories and snapshot repositories.

A release repository contains stable and finalized versions of artifacts. These artifacts are considered to be production-ready and are typically used in the final stages of the software development lifecycle.

On the other hand, a snapshot repository contains unstable and evolving versions of artifacts. These artifacts are usually used during the development and testing phases of a project. Snapshot artifacts have version numbers that end with the suffix "-SNAPSHOT" to indicate that they are not final releases.

Both release and snapshot repositories have a hierarchical structure based on the groupId, artifactId, and version of the artifacts. The groupId represents the group or organization that owns the artifact, the artifactId represents the name of the artifact, and the version represents the specific version of the artifact.

5.1.4 Repository Configuration

To work with Maven repositories, you need to configure them in your project's POM file. The POM file contains a *<repositories>* section where you can define the remote repositories that Maven should use.

Each repository is defined using the *<repository>* element, which contains the URL of the repository and other optional configuration parameters. Maven uses the URL to access the repository and retrieve the required artifacts.

Here is an example of how to configure a remote repository in the POM file:

```
<repositories>
  <repository>
    <id>my-repo</id>
    <url>https://example.com/maven-repo</url>
    <releases>
      <enabled>true</enabled>
    </releases>
    <snapshots>
      <enabled>false</enabled>
    </snapshots>
  </repository>
</repositories>
```

In this example, we define a repository with the ID "my-repo" and the URL "https://example.com/maven-repo". We also specify that only releases should be enabled and snapshots should be disabled.

By configuring remote repositories in your POM file, you can easily manage and control the dependencies and plugins used in your project. Maven will automatically download the required artifacts from the specified repositories and make them available for your project's build process.

5.1.5 Proxy Settings

In some cases, you may need to configure proxy settings to access remote repositories. Proxy settings are required when you are working behind a firewall or when your network requires a proxy server to access the internet.

Maven allows you to configure proxy settings in the *settings.xml* file, which is located in the *.m2* directory in your user's home directory. The *settings.xml* file contains various configuration options for Maven, including proxy settings.

To configure proxy settings, you need to add the *<proxies>* section in the *settings.xml* file. Within the *<proxies>* section, you can define one or more *<proxy>* elements, each representing a proxy server.

Here is an example of how to configure proxy settings in the *settings.xml* file:

```
<settings>
  <proxies>
    <proxy>
      <id>my-proxy</id>
      <active>true</active>
      <protocol>http</protocol>
      <host>proxy.example.com</host>
      <port>8080</port>
      <nonProxyHosts>localhost|127.0.0.1</nonProxyHosts>
    </proxy>
  </proxies>
</settings>
```

In this example, we define a proxy with the ID "my-proxy" and the URL "http://proxy.example.com:8080". We also specify that the proxy should be active and only used for the "http" protocol. The *<nonProxyHosts>* element allows you to specify a list of hosts that should bypass the proxy.

By configuring proxy settings, Maven will be able to access remote repositories through the specified proxy server, allowing you to download the required artifacts for your projects.

5.1.6 Conclusion

Maven repositories are an essential part of the Maven ecosystem. They provide a centralized location for storing and retrieving artifacts, making it easier to manage dependencies and plugins in your projects. By understanding how repositories work and how to configure them, you can effectively leverage the power of Maven to build and manage your projects.

5.2 Configuring Local and Remote Repositories

In Apache Maven, repositories play a crucial role in managing dependencies and artifacts. A repository is a location where Maven stores and retrieves project dependencies and artifacts. There are two types of repositories: local repositories and remote repositories.

5.2.1 Local Repository

The local repository is a directory on your local machine where Maven stores all the project dependencies and artifacts that it downloads from remote repositories. By default, the local repository is located in the *.m2* directory in your user's home directory. Maven automatically creates this directory when you run it for the first time.

The local repository acts as a cache for dependencies and artifacts, allowing Maven to work offline once the dependencies are downloaded. It also ensures that the dependencies are available for future builds, eliminating the need to download them again.

To configure the location of the local repository, you can modify the *settings.xml* file located in the *conf* directory of your Maven installation. Within the *<settings>* element, you can specify the *<localRepository>* element with the desired path to the local repository. For example:

```
<settings>
  ...
  <localRepository>/path/to/local/repository</localReposito
ry>
  ...
</settings>
```

By customizing the local repository location, you can have multiple Maven installations on the same machine, each with its own local repository.

5.2.2 Remote Repository

A remote repository is a repository that is hosted on a remote server and contains dependencies and artifacts that are not available in the local repository. Maven uses remote repositories to download dependencies and artifacts that are required for building the project.

By default, Maven is configured to use the Maven Central Repository as the primary remote repository. The Maven Central Repository is a public repository that hosts a vast collection of open-source libraries and artifacts. However, you can also configure Maven to use other remote repositories, such as third-party repositories or private repositories.

To configure remote repositories, you can modify the *pom.xml* file of your project. Within the *<repositories>* element, you can define one or more *<repository>* elements, each specifying the URL of the remote repository. For example:

```
<project>
  ...
  <repositories>
    <repository>
      <id>central</id>
      <url>https://repo.maven.apache.org/maven2</url>
    </repository>
    <repository>
      <id>third-party</id>
      <url>https://example.com/maven-repo</url>
    </repository>
  </repositories>
  ...
</project>
```

In the above example, two remote repositories are defined: the Maven Central Repository and a third-party repository hosted at *https://example.com/maven-repo*. Maven will search these repositories for any dependencies or artifacts that are required by the project.

5.2.3 Repository Authentication

In some cases, remote repositories may require authentication to access their contents. Maven provides a way to configure repository authentication in the *settings.xml* file.

Within the *<servers>* element of the *settings.xml* file, you can define one or more *<server>* elements, each specifying the credentials for a remote repository. For example:

```
<settings>
  ...
  <servers>
    <server>
      <id>central</id>
      <username>your-username</username>
      <password>your-password</password>
    </server>
    <server>
      <id>third-party</id>
      <username>your-username</username>
      <password>your-password</password>
    </server>
  </servers>
  ...
</settings>
```

In the above example, the *<id>* element corresponds to the *<id>* element of the *<repository>* in the *pom.xml* file. Maven will use the specified credentials when accessing the remote repositories.

5.2.4 Repository Mirrors

Maven also supports the concept of repository mirrors, which allows you to redirect Maven to use a different remote repository for downloading dependencies and artifacts. This can be useful in situations where you want to use a mirror repository to improve download speeds or to use a local mirror for internal dependencies.

To configure repository mirrors, you can modify the *settings.xml* file. Within the *<mirrors>* element, you can define one or more *<mirror>* elements, each specifying the URL of the mirror repository. For example:

```
<settings>
  ...
  <mirrors>
    <mirror>
      <id>mirror</id>
      <url>https://example.com/maven-mirror</url>
      <mirrorOf>central</mirrorOf>
    </mirror>
  </mirrors>
  ...
</settings>
```

In the above example, a mirror repository is defined with the URL *https://example.com/maven-mirror*, and it is configured to mirror the Maven Central Repository (*central*). Maven will use the mirror repository instead of the original repository for downloading dependencies and artifacts.

5.2.5 Repository Caching

Maven caches the artifacts it downloads from remote repositories in the local repository. This caching mechanism allows Maven to avoid downloading the same artifacts multiple times, improving build performance.

However, there may be situations where you want to force Maven to update the cached artifacts and download the latest versions from the remote repositories. You can achieve this by using the *-U* or *--update-snapshots* command-line option when running Maven. For example:

```
mvn clean install -U
```

The *-U* option tells Maven to check for updated snapshots and release versions of dependencies and artifacts and download them if necessary.

Conclusion

Configuring local and remote repositories is an essential aspect of working with Apache Maven. By understanding how to customize the local repository location, define remote repositories, configure authentication, and use repository mirrors, you can effectively manage dependencies and artifacts in your Maven projects.

5.3 Publishing Artifacts to a Repository

Once you have developed your project using Apache Maven, you may want to share your project with others or make it available for use in other projects. One way to achieve this is by publishing your project artifacts to a repository. In this section, we will explore how to publish artifacts to a repository using Apache Maven.

5.3.1 Introduction to Artifacts

Before we dive into publishing artifacts, let's first understand what artifacts are in the context of Apache Maven. In Maven, an artifact is a file that is produced by a project and is meant to be used by other projects. Examples of artifacts include JAR files, WAR files, and POM files. These artifacts contain the compiled code, resources, and metadata necessary for other projects to use or consume.

5.3.2 Configuring the Maven Repository

Before you can publish your artifacts, you need to configure the repository where you want to publish them. Maven supports various types of repositories, including local repositories, remote repositories, and third-party repositories.

5.3.2.1 Local Repository

The local repository is a local file system directory on your machine where Maven stores all the artifacts that it downloads or installs. By default, the local repository is located in the *.m2/repository* directory in your user's home directory. To publish artifacts to the local repository, you simply need to build your project using the *mvn install* command. Maven will then copy the artifacts to the local repository.

5.3.2.2 Remote Repository

A remote repository is a repository that is hosted on a remote server and can be accessed over the network. To publish artifacts to a remote repository, you need to configure the repository URL and authentication credentials in your project's POM file. Maven provides the *distributionManagement* element in the POM file to specify the remote repository details. Once configured, you can use the *mvn deploy* command to publish your artifacts to the remote repository.

5.3.3 Publishing Artifacts to the Local Repository

Publishing artifacts to the local repository is a straightforward process. When you build your project using the *mvn install* command, Maven will automatically copy the project artifacts to the local repository. This allows other projects on your machine to use the artifacts as dependencies.

To publish your artifacts to the local repository, navigate to your project's root directory in the command line and execute the following command:

```
mvn install
```

Maven will compile your project, run any tests, and package the artifacts. Once the build is successful, Maven will copy the artifacts to the local repository. You can then use these artifacts in other projects by specifying them as dependencies in the POM file.

5.3.4 Publishing Artifacts to a Remote Repository

Publishing artifacts to a remote repository requires some additional configuration. First, you need to specify the remote repository details in your project's POM file using the *distributionManagement* element. Here's an example of how to configure a remote repository:

```
<distributionManagement>
  <repository>
    <id>my-remote-repo</id>
    <url>https://example.com/repository</url>
  </repository>
</distributionManagement>
```

In the above example, we have specified the repository ID as "my-remote-repo" and the repository URL as "https://example.com/repository". You should replace these values with the actual ID and URL of your remote repository.

Once you have configured the remote repository, you can use the *mvn deploy* command to publish your artifacts. Maven will build your project, package the artifacts, and upload them to the remote repository. You will need to provide the appropriate authentication credentials when prompted.

```
mvn deploy
```

Maven will prompt you for the username and password to authenticate with the remote repository. Once authenticated, Maven will upload the artifacts to the specified repository.

5.3.5 Verifying Published Artifacts

After publishing your artifacts to a repository, it is important to verify that they have been successfully uploaded. You can do this by navigating to the repository URL in a web browser and checking if the artifacts are present.

For a local repository, you can navigate to the *.m2/repository* directory on your machine and verify that the artifacts are present in the appropriate directory structure.

For a remote repository, you can access the repository URL in a web browser and browse the directory structure to locate your artifacts. If the artifacts are present, it means that they have been successfully published.

5.3.6 Conclusion

Publishing artifacts to a repository is an essential step in sharing your project with others and making it available for use in other projects. In this section, we explored how to publish artifacts to both local and remote repositories using Apache Maven. We learned how to configure the repository, publish artifacts to the local repository, and publish artifacts to a remote repository. By following these steps, you can effectively share your project artifacts and collaborate with other developers using Apache Maven.

5.4 Using Third-Party Repositories

In addition to local and remote repositories, Maven also allows you to use third-party repositories to access external dependencies that are not available in the default repositories. Third-party repositories are external repositories maintained by individuals or organizations that host their own libraries or artifacts.

Using third-party repositories in Maven is a straightforward process. You simply need to configure the repository in your project's POM file or in your Maven settings.xml file. Maven will then search for dependencies in the specified third-party repository along with the default repositories.

5.4.1 Configuring Third-Party Repositories

To configure a third-party repository in your project's POM file, you need to add the repository element within the repositories element. The repository element consists of the id, name, URL, and layout attributes.

Here's an example of how to configure a third-party repository in your POM file:

```
<repositories>
  <repository>
    <id>my-third-party-repo</id>
    <name>My Third-Party Repository</name>
    <url>https://example.com/maven-repo</url>
    <layout>default</layout>
  </repository>
</repositories>
```

In the above example, we have configured a third-party repository with the id "my-third-party-repo", name "My Third-Party Repository", URL "https://example.com/maven-repo", and layout "default". Make sure to replace the URL with the actual URL of the third-party repository you want to use.

Alternatively, you can configure third-party repositories in your Maven settings.xml file. The settings.xml file is located in the conf directory of your Maven installation. Open the file and add the following configuration within the repositories element:

```
<repositories>
  <repository>
    <id>my-third-party-repo</id>
    <name>My Third-Party Repository</name>
    <url>https://example.com/maven-repo</url>
    <layout>default</layout>
  </repository>
</repositories>
```

Save the settings.xml file after adding the repository configuration.

5.4.2 Resolving Dependencies from Third-Party Repositories

Once you have configured a third-party repository, Maven will automatically search for dependencies in that repository when you build your project. If a dependency is not found in the default repositories, Maven will check the configured third-party repositories to resolve the dependency.

Maven follows a specific order when resolving dependencies. It first checks the local repository, then the remote repositories specified in the POM file, and finally the third-party repositories configured in the POM file or settings.xml file. If the dependency is found in any of these repositories, Maven will download it and include it in your project.

If a dependency is not found in any of the configured repositories, Maven will display an error message indicating that the dependency could not be resolved. In such cases, you may need to check the repository configuration and ensure that the dependency is available in the specified third-party repository.

5.4.3 Best Practices for Using Third-Party Repositories

When using third-party repositories in Maven, it is important to follow some best practices to ensure smooth dependency resolution and avoid potential issues:

1. **Verify the reliability of the repository**: Before adding a third-party repository, make sure it is reliable and maintained by a trusted source. Unreliable or outdated repositories may contain outdated or malicious dependencies, which can cause security vulnerabilities or compatibility issues in your project.

2. **Use reputable third-party repositories**: Whenever possible, use well-known and reputable third-party repositories. These repositories are more likely to have a wide range of high-quality dependencies and are regularly maintained and updated.

3. **Specify repository versions**: If a third-party repository provides multiple versions of the same dependency, it is a good practice to specify the version you want to use in your POM file. This ensures that your project always uses the desired version of the dependency, even if newer versions are available in the repository.

4. **Regularly update repository configurations**: Keep track of the third-party repositories used in your project and periodically check for updates or changes in their configurations. Repository URLs or layouts may change over time, and it is important to update your project's configuration accordingly to avoid dependency resolution issues.

5. **Document third-party dependencies**: When using third-party repositories, it is essential to document the dependencies and their sources in your project's documentation or README file. This helps other developers understand the external dependencies used in

your project and allows them to configure their own environments accordingly.

By following these best practices, you can effectively use third-party repositories in Maven and ensure smooth dependency resolution for your projects. Remember to regularly review and update your repository configurations to maintain a reliable and secure development environment.

6 Managing Builds with Maven

6.1 Understanding the Maven Build Lifecycle

In Apache Maven, the build process is organized into a series of well-defined phases, known as the Maven Build Lifecycle. Each phase represents a specific stage in the build process, and Maven executes these phases in a predefined order. Understanding the Maven Build Lifecycle is crucial for effectively managing and customizing your project's build process.

6.1.1 The Three Build Lifecycles

The Maven Build Lifecycle consists of three main lifecycles: the default lifecycle, the clean lifecycle, and the site lifecycle.

6.1.1.1 The Default Lifecycle

The default lifecycle is the most commonly used lifecycle in Maven. It consists of the following phases:

1. **validate**: Validates the project structure and configuration.
2. **compile**: Compiles the project's source code.
3. **test**: Runs unit tests against the compiled source code.
4. **package**: Packages the compiled code into a distributable format, such as a JAR or WAR file.
5. **verify**: Performs any checks to ensure the package is valid and meets quality standards.
6. **install**: Installs the package into the local Maven repository for use by other projects.
7. **deploy**: Deploys the package to a remote repository for sharing with other developers or projects.

By default, Maven executes all these phases in order when you run the *mvn install* command. However, you can also execute individual phases or customize the order of execution using Maven's command-line options or by modifying the project's POM file.

6.1.1.2 The Clean Lifecycle

The clean lifecycle is responsible for cleaning up artifacts generated during the build process. It consists of a single phase:

1. **clean**: Deletes all files and directories generated by the previous build.

Running the *mvn clean* command removes all build artifacts, allowing you to start the build process from a clean state. This is particularly useful when you want to ensure that no remnants of previous builds interfere with the current build.

6.1.1.3 The Site Lifecycle

The site lifecycle is used for generating project documentation and reports. It consists of the following phases:

1. **pre-site**: Executes any necessary pre-processing before generating the site.
2. **site**: Generates the project's site documentation.
3. **post-site**: Executes any necessary post-processing after generating the site.
4. **site-deploy**: Deploys the generated site to a remote location for sharing with other developers or users.

The site lifecycle is optional and is typically used for projects that require extensive documentation or reporting. Running the *mvn site* command generates the project's site documentation and reports.

6.1.2 Customizing the Build Lifecycle

Maven allows you to customize the build lifecycle by binding additional goals to existing phases or creating entirely new phases. This flexibility enables you to tailor the build process to meet your project's specific requirements.

6.1.2.1 Binding Goals to Phases

You can bind additional goals to existing phases by configuring the *<executions>* element within a plugin's configuration in the POM file. By doing so, Maven will automatically execute the bound goals during the corresponding phase.

For example, if you want to run additional tests during the *test* phase, you can configure the Surefire plugin as follows:

```
<build>
  <plugins>
    <plugin>
      <groupId>org.apache.maven.plugins</groupId>
      <artifactId>maven-surefire-plugin</artifactId>
      <version>3.0.0</version>
      <executions>
        <execution>
          <id>additional-tests</id>
          <phase>test</phase>
          <goals>
            <goal>test</goal>
          </goals>
        </execution>
      </executions>
    </plugin>
  </plugins>
</build>
```

In this example, the Surefire plugin's *test* goal is bound to the *test* phase, ensuring that the additional tests are executed alongside the default unit tests.

6.1.2.2 Creating Custom Phases

In some cases, the predefined phases may not be sufficient for your project's needs. Maven allows you to create custom phases by configuring the *<execution>* element within the *<executions>* element of a plugin.

To create a custom phase, you need to define a unique identifier for the phase and specify the goals to be executed during that phase. You can then bind the custom phase to an existing phase or define it as a standalone phase.

For example, to create a custom phase called *custom-package* that packages the project's code in a specific way, you can configure the Maven JAR plugin as follows:

```
<build>
  <plugins>
    <plugin>
      <groupId>org.apache.maven.plugins</groupId>
      <artifactId>maven-jar-plugin</artifactId>
      <version>3.2.0</version>
      <executions>
        <execution>
          <id>custom-package</id>
          <phase>package</phase>
          <goals>
            <goal>jar</goal>
          </goals>
        </execution>
      </executions>
    </plugin>
  </plugins>
</build>
```

In this example, the Maven JAR plugin's *jar* goal is bound to the custom phase *custom-package*, which is executed during the *package* phase.

6.1.3 Working with Profiles

Maven profiles allow you to customize the build process based on different environments or project requirements. A profile is a set of configuration values that can be activated or deactivated based on certain conditions.

To define a profile, you need to add a *<profile>* element within the *<profiles>* element in the POM file. You can specify the activation conditions for the profile, such as the presence of a specific system property or the value of an environment variable.

Within a profile, you can configure various aspects of the build, such as plugin configurations, dependencies, and build properties. When a profile is activated, Maven applies the configuration defined within that profile.

Profiles can be activated explicitly using the *-P* command-line option followed by the profile identifier, or they can be activated implicitly based on the activation conditions specified in the POM file.

6.1.4 Using Maven in Continuous Integration

Maven integrates seamlessly with continuous integration (CI) systems, allowing you to automate the build, test, and deployment processes. CI systems such as Jenkins, Travis CI, and Bamboo can be configured to execute Maven commands as part of the build pipeline.

By leveraging Maven's build lifecycle and plugin system, you can define CI jobs that perform tasks such as compiling the code, running tests, generating reports, and deploying artifacts to repositories. This ensures that your project is continuously built, tested, and delivered in a consistent and reliable manner.

To use Maven in a CI environment, you need to configure the CI system to execute the appropriate Maven commands, such as *mvn clean install* or *mvn test*, depending on your project's requirements. You can also configure the CI system to trigger builds automatically whenever changes are pushed to the version control system.

Maven's integration with CI systems simplifies the process of building and deploying projects, enabling teams to collaborate effectively and deliver high-quality software in a timely manner.

Conclusion

Understanding the Maven Build Lifecycle is essential for effectively managing and customizing your project's build process. By familiarizing yourself with the default, clean, and site lifecycles, you can leverage Maven's powerful features to build, test, and deploy your projects efficiently. Additionally, customizing the build lifecycle, working with profiles, and integrating Maven with CI systems further enhance your ability to automate and streamline the development process.

6.2 Customizing the Build Lifecycle

In Apache Maven, the build lifecycle is a sequence of phases that are executed in a specific order to build and package a project. By default, Maven provides a set of predefined build lifecycle phases such as compile, test, package, install, and deploy. However, there may be cases where you need to customize the build lifecycle to meet the specific requirements of your project. Maven allows you to do this by defining your own build lifecycle and configuring it according to your needs.

6.2.1 Defining Custom Build Lifecycle Phases

To define a custom build lifecycle, you need to create a new plugin and configure it in your project's POM (Project Object Model) file. The plugin will define the new build lifecycle phases and the goals associated with each phase.

Here's an example of how you can define a custom build lifecycle:

```
<build>
  <plugins>
    <plugin>
      <groupId>com.example</groupId>
      <artifactId>custom-plugin</artifactId>
      <version>1.0.0</version>
      <executions>
        <execution>
          <id>custom-lifecycle</id>
          <phase>custom-phase</phase>
          <goals>
            <goal>custom-goal</goal>
          </goals>
        </execution>
      </executions>
    </plugin>
  </plugins>
</build>
```

In the above example, we define a custom plugin with the artifactId "custom-plugin" and version "1.0.0". Inside the plugin configuration, we define an execution with an id "custom-lifecycle" and a phase "custom-phase". We also specify a goal "custom-goal" that will be executed during the "custom-phase" of the build lifecycle.

6.2.2 Configuring Custom Build Lifecycle Phases

Once you have defined the custom build lifecycle phases, you can configure them to execute specific tasks or goals. Maven provides a wide range of plugins that can be used to perform various tasks during the build process. You can configure these plugins to execute their goals at specific phases of the custom build lifecycle.

To configure a plugin for a custom build lifecycle phase, you need to specify the plugin and its goals inside the execution block of the custom plugin configuration. Here's an example:

```
<build>
  <plugins>
    <plugin>
      <groupId>com.example</groupId>
      <artifactId>custom-plugin</artifactId>
      <version>1.0.0</version>
      <executions>
        <execution>
          <id>custom-lifecycle</id>
          <phase>custom-phase</phase>
          <goals>
            <goal>custom-goal</goal>
          </goals>
        </execution>
      </executions>
      <configuration>
        <plugins>
          <plugin>
            <groupId>org.apache.maven.plugins</groupId>
            <artifactId>maven-compiler-plugin</artifactId>
            <version>3.8.1</version>
            <configuration>
              <source>1.8</source>
              <target>1.8</target>
            </configuration>
          </plugin>
        </plugins>
      </configuration>
    </plugin>
  </plugins>
</build>
```

In the above example, we configure the Maven Compiler Plugin to execute during the "custom-phase" of the build lifecycle. We specify the plugin's groupId, artifactId, and version, and inside the configuration block, we set the source and target versions for the compiler.

6.2.3 Executing Custom Build Lifecycle Phases

To execute the custom build lifecycle phases, you can use the Maven command line interface (CLI) or an integrated development environment (IDE) that supports Maven. When you run the build command, Maven will execute the custom build lifecycle phases in the specified order.

For example, if you have defined a custom build lifecycle phase called "custom-phase", you can execute it using the following command:

```
mvn custom-phase
```

Maven will execute all the goals associated with the "custom-phase" in the order specified in the POM file.

6.2.4 Benefits of Customizing the Build Lifecycle

Customizing the build lifecycle in Maven provides several benefits. It allows you to tailor the build process to meet the specific requirements of your project. You can define new build lifecycle phases and configure them to execute tasks or goals that are specific to your project.

By customizing the build lifecycle, you can automate repetitive tasks, enforce coding standards, perform static code analysis, generate reports, and more. This helps in improving the overall quality and efficiency of the build process.

Additionally, customizing the build lifecycle allows you to integrate other tools and technologies seamlessly into your build process. You can execute scripts, invoke external tools, or perform any other custom actions during the build.

6.2.5 Best Practices for Customizing the Build Lifecycle

When customizing the build lifecycle in Maven, it is important to follow some best practices to ensure a smooth and maintainable build process. Here are a few recommendations:

1. Keep the build lifecycle simple and focused: Define only the necessary build lifecycle phases and goals that are specific to your project. Avoid adding unnecessary complexity to the build process.

2. Use existing plugins whenever possible: Instead of creating custom plugins, try to leverage existing plugins provided by the Maven ecosystem. This helps in reusing well-tested and widely adopted solutions.

3. Document the custom build lifecycle: Clearly document the purpose and functionality of each custom build lifecycle phase and goal. This helps in understanding and maintaining the build process in the future.

4. Test and validate the custom build lifecycle: Before integrating the custom build lifecycle into your project, thoroughly test and validate it to ensure that it works as expected. Use sample projects or prototypes to verify the functionality.

By following these best practices, you can effectively customize the build lifecycle in Maven and optimize the build process for your project.

Conclusion

Customizing the build lifecycle in Apache Maven allows you to tailor the build process to meet the specific requirements of your project. By defining custom build lifecycle phases and configuring them with plugins and goals, you can automate tasks, enforce coding standards, integrate external tools, and improve the overall quality and efficiency of the build process. Following best practices ensures a maintainable and effective custom build lifecycle.

6.3 Working with Profiles

Profiles are a powerful feature in Apache Maven that allow you to customize the build process based on different environments, such as development, testing, and production. With profiles, you can define specific configurations, dependencies, and plugins that are only activated under certain conditions. This flexibility enables you to manage different build configurations without duplicating or modifying the main POM file.

6.3.1 Introduction to Profiles

Profiles in Maven are defined within the *<profiles>* element in the POM file. Each profile can have its own set of configurations, dependencies, and plugins. Profiles can be activated based on various criteria, such as the presence of a specific system property, the operating system, or the value of a specific environment variable.

To define a profile, you need to specify an *<id>* for the profile and include the desired configurations within the *<profile>* element. Here's an example of a profile that configures the compiler plugin to use Java 11:

```
<profiles>
  <profile>
    <id>java11</id>
    <activation>
      <jdk>11</jdk>
    </activation>
    <build>
      <plugins>
        <plugin>
          <groupId>org.apache.maven.plugins</groupId>
          <artifactId>maven-compiler-plugin</artifactId>
          <version>3.8.1</version>
          <configuration>
            <source>11</source>
            <target>11</target>
          </configuration>
        </plugin>
      </plugins>
    </build>
  </profile>
</profiles>
```

In this example, the profile is activated when the JDK version is 11. When the profile is active, the compiler plugin is configured to use Java 11 as the source and target version.

6.3.2 Activating Profiles

Profiles can be activated in several ways. The most common method is through the command line using the *-P* or *--activate-profiles* option followed by a comma-separated list of profile IDs. For example, to activate the *java11* profile from the previous example, you would run the following command:

```
mvn clean install -P java11
```

You can also activate profiles based on the presence or absence of a specific system property using the *<activation>* element. For example, to activate a profile when the *environment* system property is set to *dev*, you can define the profile as follows:

```
<profiles>
  <profile>
    <id>dev</id>
    <activation>
      <property>
        <name>environment</name>
        <value>dev</value>
      </property>
    </activation>
    <!-- Profile configurations -->
  </profile>
</profiles>
```

In this case, the profile will be activated when the `environment` system property is set to `dev`. You can activate this profile by passing the system property as a command-line argument:

```
mvn clean install -Denvironment=dev
```

6.3.3 Profile Inheritance

Profiles in Maven can also inherit configurations from other profiles. This allows you to define common configurations in a parent profile and override or extend them in child profiles. To inherit configurations from a parent profile, you can use the `<parent>` element within the `<profile>` element.

Here's an example that demonstrates profile inheritance:

```
<profiles>
  <profile>
    <id>parent</id>
    <build>
      <plugins>
        <plugin>
          <groupId>org.apache.maven.plugins</groupId>
          <artifactId>maven-compiler-plugin</artifactId>
          <version>3.8.1</version>
          <configuration>
            <source>11</source>
            <target>11</target>
          </configuration>
        </plugin>
      </plugins>
    </build>
  </profile>
  <profile>
    <id>child</id>
    <parent>
      <id>parent</id>
    </parent>
    <build>
      <plugins>
        <plugin>
          <groupId>org.apache.maven.plugins</groupId>
          <artifactId>maven-surefire-plugin</artifactId>
          <version>3.0.0-M5</version>
          <configuration>
            <includes>
              <include>**/*Test.java</include>
            </includes>
          </configuration>
        </plugin>
      </plugins>
    </build>
  </profile>
</profiles>
```

In this example, the *child* profile inherits the compiler plugin configuration from the *parent* profile. Additionally, it adds a configuration for the Surefire plugin to include only test classes ending with “Test.java”. By using profile inheritance, you can avoid duplicating common configurations across multiple profiles.

6.3.4 Overriding Configurations

Profiles in Maven allow you to override configurations defined in the main POM file or in parent profiles. This can be useful when you need to customize certain configurations for a specific profile. To override a configuration, simply redefine it within the profile.

Here's an example that demonstrates configuration overriding:

```
<profiles>
  <profile>
    <id>dev</id>
    <build>
      <plugins>
        <plugin>
          <groupId>org.apache.maven.plugins</groupId>
          <artifactId>maven-compiler-plugin</artifactId>
          <version>3.8.1</version>
          <configuration>
            <source>11</source>
            <target>11</target>
          </configuration>
        </plugin>
      </plugins>
    </build>
  </profile>
  <profile>
    <id>prod</id>
    <build>
      <plugins>
        <plugin>
          <groupId>org.apache.maven.plugins</groupId>
          <artifactId>maven-compiler-plugin</artifactId>
          <version>3.8.1</version>
          <configuration>
            <source>8</source>
            <target>8</target>
          </configuration>
        </plugin>
      </plugins>
    </build>
  </profile>
</profiles>
```

In this example, the *dev* profile configures the compiler plugin to use Java 11, while the *prod* profile overrides the configuration to use Java 8. When you activate the *dev* profile, Maven will use Java 11 for compilation, and when you activate the *prod* profile, Maven will use Java 8.

6.3.5 Using Profiles for Environment-Specific Dependencies

One common use case for profiles in Maven is managing environment-specific dependencies. For example, you may have different database drivers or API clients depending on the environment. With profiles, you can define different sets of dependencies for each environment and activate the appropriate profile based on the target environment.

Here's an example that demonstrates using profiles for environment-specific dependencies:

```
<profiles>
  <profile>
    <id>dev</id>
    <dependencies>
      <dependency>
        <groupId>com.example</groupId>
        <artifactId>dev-database-driver</artifactId>
        <version>1.0.0</version>
      </dependency>
    </dependencies>
  </profile>
  <profile>
    <id>prod</id>
    <dependencies>
      <dependency>
        <groupId>com.example</groupId>
        <artifactId>prod-database-driver</artifactId>
        <version>1.0.0</version>
      </dependency>
    </dependencies>
  </profile>
</profiles>
```

In this example, the *dev* profile includes the *dev-database-driver* dependency, while the *prod* profile includes the *prod-database-driver* dependency. By activating the appropriate profile, Maven will resolve and include the corresponding dependency in the build.

Profiles in Maven provide a flexible and powerful way to customize the build process based on different environments or conditions. By leveraging profiles, you can easily manage different configurations, dependencies, and plugins without modifying the main POM file. This allows for greater flexibility and maintainability in your Maven projects.

6.4 Using Maven in Continuous Integration

Continuous Integration (CI) is a software development practice that involves regularly integrating code changes from multiple developers into a shared repository. The goal of CI is to detect and resolve integration issues early in the development process. Maven, with its powerful build and dependency management capabilities, is a popular choice for implementing CI workflows.

In this section, we will explore how Maven can be used in a CI environment to automate the build, test, and deployment processes. We will discuss the benefits of using Maven in CI, the different CI tools that integrate with Maven, and best practices for setting up a CI pipeline with Maven.

6.4.1 Benefits of Using Maven in CI

Using Maven in a CI environment offers several benefits that contribute to the overall efficiency and reliability of the development process. Here are some key advantages:

Simplified Build Configuration

Maven provides a declarative approach to build configuration through its Project Object Model (POM). This makes it easier to define and manage build settings, dependencies, and plugins. With Maven, developers can focus on writing code rather than spending time on complex build configurations.

Dependency Management

One of the core features of Maven is its robust dependency management system. Maven automatically resolves and downloads project dependencies from remote repositories, ensuring that the correct versions are used. This simplifies the process of managing dependencies in a CI environment, where multiple projects may have interdependencies.

Consistent Build Environment

Maven ensures that the build environment is consistent across different machines and CI servers. By defining the build settings in the POM, developers can ensure that the build process is reproducible and consistent, regardless of the environment in which it is executed. This reduces the chances of build failures due to environment-specific issues.

Automated Testing

Maven integrates seamlessly with popular testing frameworks such as JUnit and TestNG. It provides plugins for running unit tests, generating test reports, and measuring code coverage. By incorporating testing into the CI pipeline, developers can catch bugs and issues early, leading to higher quality software.

Continuous Deployment

Maven can be used to automate the deployment of artifacts to remote repositories or application servers. By configuring the appropriate plugins, developers can streamline the deployment process and ensure that the latest version of the software is always available for testing or production environments.

6.4.2 CI Tools Integration with Maven

Maven is widely supported by various CI tools, making it easy to integrate Maven into your CI workflow. Here are some popular CI tools that have native support for Maven:

Jenkins

Jenkins is a widely used open-source CI/CD tool that provides extensive support for Maven. Jenkins can automatically trigger builds whenever changes are pushed to the repository, and it can execute Maven goals as part of the build process. Jenkins also provides built-in support for generating test reports and code coverage reports using Maven plugins.

Bamboo

Bamboo is a CI/CD tool from Atlassian that offers seamless integration with Maven. Bamboo can be configured to monitor repositories for changes and trigger builds accordingly. It provides built-in support for Maven builds and can generate detailed build reports and artifacts.

TeamCity

TeamCity is a powerful CI/CD server from JetBrains that supports Maven out of the box. TeamCity can automatically detect changes in the repository and trigger builds using Maven. It provides comprehensive build reports, test reports, and code coverage reports for Maven projects.

GitLab CI/CD

GitLab CI/CD is a built-in CI/CD solution provided by GitLab. It has native support for Maven and can execute Maven goals as part of the CI pipeline. GitLab CI/CD can automatically trigger builds whenever changes are pushed to the repository and provides detailed build logs and reports.

6.4.3 Best Practices for Setting up a CI Pipeline with Maven

To ensure a smooth and efficient CI workflow with Maven, it is important to follow some best practices. Here are some recommendations for setting up a CI pipeline with Maven:

Version Control Integration

Integrate your Maven project with a version control system like Git or SVN. This allows the CI tool to monitor the repository for changes and trigger builds accordingly. It also ensures that the correct version of the source code is used for each build.

Isolated Build Environment

Create an isolated build environment for each build to ensure reproducibility and avoid conflicts between different builds. This can be achieved by using virtual machines or containers. Maven's dependency management system ensures that the required dependencies are downloaded and used for each build.

Parallel Builds

Leverage the parallel build feature of Maven to speed up the build process. By configuring the appropriate settings in the POM, Maven can execute multiple build tasks in parallel, utilizing the available resources efficiently.

Automated Testing

Integrate automated testing into the CI pipeline using Maven plugins such as Surefire and Failsafe. Configure the plugins to run unit tests and integration tests as part of the build process. This helps catch bugs and issues early, ensuring the quality of the software.

Continuous Deployment

Automate the deployment process using Maven plugins such as the Maven Deploy Plugin or the Maven Cargo Plugin. Configure the plugins to deploy artifacts to remote repositories or application servers automatically. This ensures that the latest version of the software is always available for testing or production environments.

Build Notifications

Configure the CI tool to send notifications on build status and failures. This helps keep the development team informed about the build progress and allows for quick resolution of any issues that arise.

By following these best practices, you can maximize the benefits of using Maven in a CI environment and ensure a smooth and efficient development process.

Conclusion

In this section, we explored how Maven can be used in a Continuous Integration (CI) environment. We discussed the benefits of using Maven in CI, the different CI tools that integrate with Maven, and best practices for setting up a CI pipeline with Maven. By leveraging Maven's powerful build and dependency management capabilities, developers can automate the build, test, and deployment processes, leading to more efficient and reliable software development.

7 Testing with Apache Maven

7.1 Introduction to Maven Testing

Testing is an essential part of software development. It helps ensure that the code behaves as expected and meets the requirements. Apache Maven provides a comprehensive testing framework that allows developers to easily write and execute tests for their projects. In this section, we will explore the different types of testing supported by Maven and how to effectively use them in your projects.

7.1.1 Unit Testing with Maven

Unit testing is the process of testing individual units or components of a software system to ensure their correctness. Maven supports unit testing through the use of various testing frameworks such as JUnit, TestNG, and Spock.

To write unit tests in Maven, you need to create a separate directory called “src/test/java” in your project’s directory structure. This directory will contain all the test classes. Maven follows a convention where the test classes should have the same package structure as the classes they are testing, but under the “test” directory.

Once you have written your unit tests, you can use Maven’s build lifecycle to execute them. Maven automatically recognizes the test classes and runs them during the “test” phase of the build lifecycle. You can execute the tests by running the following command:

```
mvn test
```

Maven will compile the test classes, execute them, and generate a report showing the test results. The report includes information such as the number of tests executed, the number of failures, and the test coverage.

7.1.2 Integration Testing with Maven

Integration testing is the process of testing the interaction between different components or modules of a software system. Maven provides support for integration testing through the use of plugins such as the Maven Failsafe Plugin.

To write integration tests in Maven, you need to create a separate directory called "src/test/java" in your project's directory structure, just like for unit tests. However, the integration tests should be placed under a different package structure, typically "it" or "integration".

Maven's Failsafe Plugin is responsible for executing the integration tests. By default, it looks for test classes with names ending in "IT" or "ITCase". You can configure the plugin to include or exclude specific tests based on your requirements.

To execute the integration tests, you can use the following command:

```
mvn verify
```

The "verify" phase of the build lifecycle is responsible for executing the integration tests. Maven will compile the integration test classes, start the necessary infrastructure (e.g., databases, web servers), execute the tests, and generate a report showing the test results.

7.1.3 Code Coverage and Quality Analysis

Code coverage is a measure of how much of your code is being tested by your test suite. It helps identify areas of your code that are not adequately covered by tests. Maven integrates with code coverage tools such as JaCoCo and Cobertura to provide code coverage reports.

To enable code coverage analysis in Maven, you need to configure the code coverage plugin in your project's POM file. The plugin will instrument your code during the build process and collect coverage data while executing the tests.

Once the tests are executed, you can generate a code coverage report by running the following command:

```
mvn jacoco:report
```

Maven will generate a report showing the code coverage metrics, such as the percentage of lines, branches, and methods covered by tests. This report can help you identify areas of your code that need additional testing.

In addition to code coverage, Maven also integrates with static code analysis tools such as SonarQube and PMD. These tools analyze your code for potential bugs, code smells, and other quality issues. By configuring the appropriate plugins in your project's POM file, you can generate reports that provide insights into the quality of your code.

Conclusion

Maven provides a robust testing framework that allows developers to easily write and execute tests for their projects. By leveraging Maven's support for unit testing, integration testing, code coverage, and quality analysis, you can ensure the reliability and quality of your software. Incorporating testing into your development process not only helps catch bugs early but also improves the maintainability and stability of your codebase.

7.2 Unit Testing with Maven

Unit testing is an essential part of the software development process. It allows developers to verify the correctness of individual units of code, such as methods or classes, in isolation. Apache Maven provides a robust framework for automating and managing unit tests within a project.

7.2.1 Introduction to Unit Testing

Unit testing is a software testing technique where individual units of code are tested to ensure that they function correctly. These units are typically small and isolated, such as methods or classes. The goal of unit testing is to identify and fix bugs early in the development process, ensuring that each unit of code behaves as expected.

Unit tests are typically written by developers themselves and are executed frequently during the development process. They help to catch bugs and regressions, ensuring that changes to the codebase do not introduce new issues. Unit tests also serve as documentation, providing examples of how to use the code and its expected behavior.

7.2.2 Setting Up Unit Tests in Maven

Apache Maven provides a standardized way to configure and execute unit tests within a project. To set up unit tests in Maven, you need to follow these steps:

1. Create a separate directory for your unit tests. By convention, Maven expects unit tests to be placed in the *src/test/java* directory.
2. Write your unit tests using a testing framework such as JUnit or TestNG. These frameworks provide a set of annotations and assertions to define and verify test cases.
3. Configure the Maven Surefire Plugin in your project's POM file. The Surefire Plugin is responsible for executing unit tests

during the build process. You can specify the test directory and testing framework to be used.

4. Run the *mvn test* command to execute the unit tests. Maven will compile the test sources, execute the tests, and generate a report with the test results.

7.2.3 Writing Unit Tests with JUnit

JUnit is one of the most popular testing frameworks for Java applications. It provides a simple and expressive API for writing unit tests. Here's an example of a basic JUnit test case:

```
import org.junit.Test;
import static org.junit.Assert.*;

public class MyMathTest {

    @Test
    public void testAddition() {
        int result = MyMath.add(2, 3);
        assertEquals(5, result);
    }

    @Test
    public void testSubtraction() {
        int result = MyMath.subtract(5, 3);
        assertEquals(2, result);
    }
}
```

In this example, we have a test class *MyMathTest* with two test methods: *testAddition* and *testSubtraction*. Each test method is annotated with *@Test*, indicating that it is a test case. Within each test method, we use assertions from the *org.junit.Assert* class to verify the expected results.

7.2.4 Running Unit Tests with Maven

Once you have written your unit tests, you can run them using the Maven Surefire Plugin. The Surefire Plugin is configured by default in the *pom.xml* file of a Maven project. To execute the unit tests, simply run the following command:

```
mvn test
```

Maven will compile the test sources, execute the tests, and generate a report with the test results. The test report is saved in the *target/surefire-reports* directory of your project. It provides detailed information about the test execution, including the number of tests run, passed, failed, and skipped.

7.2.5 Configuring Unit Tests in Maven

The Maven Surefire Plugin provides various configuration options to customize the behavior of unit tests. These options can be specified in the *pom.xml* file of your project. Here are some common configuration options:

- *includes* and *excludes*: Specify patterns to include or exclude specific test classes or methods.
- *parallel* and *threadCount*: Enable parallel execution of tests and specify the number of threads to use.
- *systemPropertyVariables*: Set system properties that can be accessed by the tests.
- *testFailureIgnore*: Ignore test failures and continue with the build process.

For example, to exclude a specific test class from execution, you can add the following configuration to your *pom.xml* file:

```
<build>
    <plugins>
        <plugin>
            <groupId>org.apache.maven.plugins</groupId>
            <artifactId>maven-surefire-plugin</artifactId>
            <configuration>
                <excludes>
                    <exclude>**/MyMathTest.java</exclude>
                </excludes>
            </configuration>
        </plugin>
    </plugins>
</build>
```

7.2.6 Generating Code Coverage Reports

Code coverage is a measure of how much of your code is being exercised by your tests. It helps identify areas of your code that are not adequately tested. Maven integrates with code coverage tools such as JaCoCo and Cobertura to generate code coverage reports.

To generate a code coverage report, you need to configure the code coverage tool in your `pom.xml` file and run the `mvn test` command. The code coverage report will be generated in the `target/site` directory of your project.

Here's an example configuration for JaCoCo:

```
<build>
    <plugins>
        <plugin>
            <groupId>org.jacoco</groupId>
            <artifactId>jacoco-maven-plugin</artifactId>
            <version>0.8.7</version>
            <executions>
                <execution>
                    <goals>
                        <goal>prepare-agent</goal>
                    </goals>
                </execution>
                <execution>
                    <id>report</id>
                    <phase>test</phase>
                    <goals>
                        <goal>report</goal>
                    </goals>
                </execution>
            </executions>
        </plugin>
    </plugins>
</build>
```

After running the `mvn test` command, you can open the generated HTML report in your web browser to view the code coverage metrics.

7.2.7 Conclusion

Unit testing is a crucial aspect of software development, and Apache Maven provides a seamless way to manage and execute unit tests within your projects. By following the conventions and using the Maven Surefire Plugin, you can easily write, run, and generate reports for your unit tests. Additionally, integrating code coverage tools like JaCoCo or Cobertura allows you to measure the effectiveness of your tests and identify areas that require further testing.

7.3 Integration Testing with Maven

Integration testing is an essential part of the software development process. It involves testing the interaction between different components or modules of an application to ensure that they work together correctly. In this section, we will explore how Apache Maven can be used to perform integration testing in your projects.

7.3.1 Introduction to Integration Testing

Integration testing is a type of testing that focuses on verifying the correct behavior of the integrated components of an application. It helps identify issues that may arise when different modules interact with each other, such as compatibility problems, communication failures, or data inconsistencies.

Integration testing is typically performed after unit testing, where individual components are tested in isolation. While unit testing ensures that each component functions correctly on its own, integration testing validates that the components work together as expected.

7.3.2 Setting Up Integration Tests in Maven

To perform integration testing with Maven, you need to set up a separate test suite specifically designed for integration tests. This suite will contain tests that exercise the interaction between different components of your application.

7.3.2.1 Creating the Integration Test Suite

To create the integration test suite, you can follow these steps:

1. Create a new directory called *src/test/java* in your Maven project.

2. Inside the *src/test/java* directory, create a package structure that mirrors the package structure of your main source code.
3. Create a new Java class that will serve as the entry point for your integration tests. This class should be placed in the same package structure as your main source code.
4. Write integration tests in this class that exercise the interaction between different components of your application.

7.3.2.2 Configuring the Maven Surefire Plugin

The Maven Surefire Plugin is responsible for executing tests in Maven projects. To configure it to run your integration tests, you need to make some modifications to your project's *pom.xml* file.

1. Add the following configuration to the *build* section of your *pom.xml* file:

```
<build>
  <plugins>
    <plugin>
      <groupId>org.apache.maven.plugins</groupId>
      <artifactId>maven-surefire-plugin</artifactId>
      <configuration>
        <includes>
          <include>**/*IT.java</include>
        </includes>
      </configuration>
    </plugin>
  </plugins>
</build>
```

This configuration tells the Surefire Plugin to include any test classes that end with *IT* (which stands for Integration Test) in the test execution.

2. By default, the Surefire Plugin runs the integration tests during the *integration-test* phase of the Maven build lifecycle. If you want to skip the integration tests, you can use the -*DskipITs* option when running Maven commands.

7.3.3 Running Integration Tests

Once you have set up your integration test suite and configured the Surefire Plugin, you can run your integration tests using Maven.

To run the integration tests, open a terminal or command prompt and navigate to the root directory of your Maven project. Then, execute the following command:

```
mvn integration-test
```

This command will execute the integration tests and generate a report of the test results. If any tests fail, Maven will provide detailed information about the failures, including stack traces and error messages.

7.3.4 Integration Testing Best Practices

When performing integration testing with Maven, it is important to follow some best practices to ensure the effectiveness and reliability of your tests.

7.3.4.1 Isolate External Dependencies

To ensure that your integration tests are reliable and repeatable, it is crucial to isolate external dependencies. This can be achieved by using techniques such as mocking or stubbing external services or using in-memory databases instead of production databases.

By isolating external dependencies, you can control the behavior of these dependencies during testing and avoid issues caused by external factors.

7.3.4.2 Use Test Data Management

Integration tests often require test data to simulate real-world scenarios. It is important to manage test data effectively to ensure consistent and reliable test results.

You can use techniques such as data seeding, database snapshots, or test data generation tools to create and manage test data for your integration tests. This will help you set up the necessary data for each test case and ensure that the data is in a known state before running the tests.

7.3.4.3 Automate Integration Tests

To ensure that integration tests are executed regularly and consistently, it is recommended to automate them as part of your build process. By integrating the execution of integration tests into your continuous integration (CI) pipeline, you can catch integration issues early and prevent them from reaching production.

Automating integration tests also allows you to run them in parallel, saving time and resources. You can use tools such as Jenkins, Travis CI, or GitLab CI/CD to automate the execution of your integration tests.

Conclusion

Integration testing plays a crucial role in ensuring the reliability and stability of your software applications. With Apache Maven, you can easily set up and execute integration tests as part of your build process. By following best practices and leveraging the power of Maven, you can improve the quality of your software and deliver more robust applications to your users.

7.4 Code Coverage and Quality Analysis

Code coverage and quality analysis are essential aspects of software development. They help ensure that the code is thoroughly tested and meets the required quality standards. Apache Maven provides several tools and plugins that can be used to measure code coverage and analyze the quality of your project.

7.4.1 Code Coverage

Code coverage is a metric that measures the percentage of code that is executed during testing. It helps identify areas of the code that are not adequately tested and may contain bugs. Maven integrates with popular code coverage tools such as JaCoCo and Cobertura to generate code coverage reports.

7.4.1.1 JaCoCo

JaCoCo is a widely used code coverage tool that provides detailed information about the code coverage of your project. To use JaCoCo with Maven, you need to configure the JaCoCo plugin in your project's POM file.

```
<build>
  <plugins>
    <plugin>
      <groupId>org.jacoco</groupId>
      <artifactId>jacoco-maven-plugin</artifactId>
      <version>0.8.7</version>
      <executions>
        <execution>
          <goals>
            <goal>prepare-agent</goal>
          </goals>
        </execution>
        <execution>
          <id>report</id>
          <phase>test</phase>
          <goals>
            <goal>report</goal>
          </goals>
        </execution>
      </executions>
    </plugin>
  </plugins>
</build>
```

The above configuration sets up the JaCoCo plugin to run during the test phase of the Maven build. It generates a code coverage report after the tests are executed. You can view the report by opening the `target/site/jacoco/index.html` file in your web browser.

7.4.1.2 Cobertura

Cobertura is another popular code coverage tool that can be integrated with Maven. To use Cobertura, you need to configure the Cobertura plugin in your project's POM file.

```
<build>
  <plugins>
    <plugin>
      <groupId>org.codehaus.mojo</groupId>
      <artifactId>cobertura-maven-plugin</artifactId>
      <version>2.7</version>
      <configuration>
        <formats>
          <format>html</format>
          <format>xml</format>
        </formats>
      </configuration>
      <executions>
        <execution>
          <phase>test</phase>
          <goals>
            <goal>cobertura</goal>
          </goals>
        </execution>
      </executions>
    </plugin>
  </plugins>
</build>
```

The above configuration sets up the Cobertura plugin to run during the test phase of the Maven build. It generates code coverage reports in both HTML and XML formats. You can view the HTML report by opening the `target/site/cobertura/index.html` file in your web browser.

7.4.2 Quality Analysis

In addition to code coverage, it is important to analyze the quality of your code. Maven integrates with various static code analysis tools that can help identify potential issues and enforce coding standards.

7.4.2.1 SonarQube

SonarQube is a popular open-source platform for continuous code quality inspection. It provides a wide range of code analysis rules and metrics to evaluate the quality of your code. To use SonarQube with Maven, you need to configure the SonarQube plugin in your project's POM file.

```
<build>
  <plugins>
    <plugin>
      <groupId>org.sonarsource.scanner.maven</groupId>
      <artifactId>sonar-maven-plugin</artifactId>
      <version>3.7.0.1746</version>
    </plugin>
  </plugins>
</build>
```

After configuring the SonarQube plugin, you need to run the following command to analyze your project:

```
mvn sonar:sonar
```

This command will analyze your code and send the results to the SonarQube server. You can then view the analysis report on the SonarQube dashboard.

7.4.2.2 Checkstyle

Checkstyle is a static code analysis tool that checks your code against a set of predefined coding standards. It helps enforce consistent coding practices and identifies potential issues. To use Checkstyle with Maven, you need to configure the Checkstyle plugin in your project's POM file.

```
<build>
  <plugins>
    <plugin>
      <groupId>org.apache.maven.plugins</groupId>
      <artifactId>maven-checkstyle-plugin</artifactId>
      <version>3.1.2</version>
      <configuration>
        <configLocation>checkstyle.xml</configLocation>
      </configuration>
      <executions>
        <execution>
          <phase>validate</phase>
          <goals>
            <goal>check</goal>
          </goals>
        </execution>
      </executions>
    </plugin>
  </plugins>
</build>
```

The above configuration sets up the Checkstyle plugin to run during the validate phase of the Maven build. It uses a Checkstyle configuration file (`checkstyle.xml`) to define the coding standards. You can customize the configuration file to match your project's coding standards.

7.4.3 Integration with Continuous Integration

Code coverage and quality analysis are often integrated into the continuous integration (CI) process. Maven can be easily integrated with popular CI servers such as Jenkins, Bamboo, and TeamCity.

By configuring your CI server to run the Maven build with code coverage and quality analysis plugins, you can ensure that every build is thoroughly tested and analyzed for quality. The CI server can generate reports and notify the development team of any issues or regressions.

Conclusion

Code coverage and quality analysis are crucial aspects of software development. Apache Maven provides a seamless integration with various code coverage and quality analysis tools. By configuring these tools in your Maven project, you can ensure that your code is thoroughly tested and meets the required quality standards.

8 Advanced Maven Concepts

8.1 Working with Multi-module Projects

In this section, we will explore the concept of multi-module projects in Apache Maven. A multi-module project is a project that consists of multiple modules, each representing a separate subproject within the main project. This approach allows for better organization and management of complex projects, as well as the ability to share resources and dependencies between modules.

8.1.1 What is a Multi-module Project?

A multi-module project is a project that is divided into multiple modules, each with its own separate directory structure and POM file. These modules can be thought of as individual projects within the main project, each with its own set of source code, resources, and dependencies.

The main advantage of using a multi-module project structure is that it allows for better organization and management of large and complex projects. By breaking down the project into smaller modules, it becomes easier to understand and maintain the codebase. Each module can focus on a specific functionality or component, making it easier to develop, test, and deploy.

8.1.2 Creating a Multi-module Project

To create a multi-module project in Maven, you need to follow a specific directory structure and configure the parent POM file accordingly.

1. Start by creating a new directory for your multi-module project. This will serve as the root directory for all the modules.

2. Inside the root directory, create a new file called *pom.xml*. This will be the parent POM file for the multi-module project.

3. In the parent POM file, define the modules by adding a `<modules>` element. Inside this element, list all the modules that are part of the project. Each module should be enclosed in a `<module>` tag.

4. Create a separate directory for each module inside the root directory. Each module directory should have its own POM file, source code, and resources.

5. In each module's POM file, specify the parent POM by adding a `<parent>` element. Inside this element, provide the `groupId`, `artifactId`, and `version` of the parent project.

6. Configure the dependencies and build settings for each module in their respective POM files.

8.1.3 Building a Multi-module Project

Building a multi-module project is similar to building a regular Maven project. However, when you build a multi-module project, Maven will build all the modules in the correct order based on their dependencies.

To build a multi-module project, navigate to the root directory of the project in the command line and execute the following command:

```
mvn clean install
```

This command will build all the modules in the correct order, resolving dependencies between modules as needed. Maven will also execute any build plugins and perform any other configured tasks.

8.1.4 Working with Dependencies in Multi-module Projects

One of the key benefits of using a multi-module project structure is the ability to share dependencies between modules. By defining dependencies in the parent POM file, you can ensure that all modules have access to the required dependencies without duplicating them in each module's POM file.

To define dependencies in the parent POM file, add a *<dependencies>* element inside the *<dependencyManagement>* section. Inside this element, list all the dependencies that are common to all modules. Each dependency should be enclosed in a *<dependency>* tag.

In each module's POM file, you can then reference these dependencies without specifying their version. Maven will automatically resolve the version from the parent POM file.

8.1.5 Benefits of Multi-module Projects

Using a multi-module project structure in Apache Maven offers several benefits:

1. **Modularity**: Breaking down a project into smaller modules makes it easier to understand and maintain the codebase. Each module can focus on a specific functionality or component, improving code organization and reusability.

2. **Dependency Management**: By defining dependencies in the parent POM file, you can ensure that all modules have access to the required dependencies without duplicating them in each module's POM file. This simplifies dependency management and reduces the risk of version conflicts.

3. **Build Order**: Maven automatically determines the correct build order for the modules based on their

dependencies. This ensures that modules are built in the correct sequence, avoiding any compilation or runtime errors.

4. **Resource Sharing**: Modules within a multi-module project can share resources, such as configuration files or test data. This promotes code reuse and reduces duplication of effort.

5. **Simplified Release Management**: With a multi-module project, it becomes easier to manage the release process. You can release all modules together as a single unit, ensuring that all dependencies are compatible and tested together.

Overall, working with multi-module projects in Apache Maven provides a structured and efficient approach to managing complex projects. It promotes modularity, simplifies dependency management, and improves code organization and reusability.

8.2 Managing Project Releases with Maven

Managing project releases is an essential aspect of software development. It involves packaging and distributing your project to end-users or other developers. Apache Maven provides a comprehensive set of tools and features to simplify the release management process. In this section, we will explore how Maven can help you effectively manage project releases.

8.2.1 Release Management Workflow

Before diving into the details of release management with Maven, let's first understand the typical workflow involved in managing project releases. The release management process usually consists of the following steps:

1. **Versioning**: Assigning a unique version number to each release is crucial for tracking changes and managing dependencies. Maven follows the Semantic Versioning scheme, where a version number consists of three parts: MAJOR.MINOR.PATCH. The MAJOR version is incremented for incompatible changes, the MINOR version for backward-compatible additions, and the PATCH version for backward-compatible bug fixes.

2. **Preparing for Release**: Before creating a release, it is essential to ensure that the project is in a stable state. This involves running tests, performing code reviews, and addressing any critical issues or bugs.

3. **Creating a Release Candidate**: Once the project is ready for release, a release candidate is created. The release candidate is a version of the project that is considered stable and ready for distribution. It is typically tested extensively to ensure its quality.

4. **Performing Release Tasks**: After the release candidate is created, various release tasks need to be performed.

These tasks may include updating version numbers, generating release documentation, creating distribution packages, and publishing artifacts to a repository.

5. **Deploying the Release**: Once the release tasks are completed, the release artifacts are deployed to a repository or distributed to end-users. This step ensures that the project is accessible to the intended audience.

6. **Post-Release Activities**: After the release is deployed, it is essential to monitor its usage, gather feedback, and address any issues that may arise. This feedback can be used to improve future releases and enhance the overall quality of the project.

8.2.2 Maven Release Plugin

Maven provides a dedicated plugin called the Maven Release Plugin to automate the release management process. The plugin simplifies the steps involved in creating and deploying releases, making the process more efficient and less error-prone.

The Maven Release Plugin follows a convention-based approach to manage releases. It uses the project's version number and SCM (Source Control Management) information to create release candidates, update version numbers, and perform other release-related tasks.

To use the Maven Release Plugin, you need to configure it in your project's POM file. The plugin configuration includes specifying the SCM connection details, release version, and development version. Additionally, you can customize the release process by configuring various goals and phases of the plugin.

Once the plugin is configured, you can initiate the release process by executing the *mvn release:prepare* command. This command prepares the project for release by creating a release candidate, updating version numbers, and performing other necessary tasks. The plugin prompts you for the release version and the next development version during this process.

After the release preparation is complete, you can execute the *mvn release:perform* command to perform the release tasks. This command builds the release artifacts, deploys them to a repository, and updates the SCM information. It also tags the release in the version control system, making it easy to track and manage different releases.

8.2.3 Best Practices for Managing Releases

Managing project releases effectively requires following best practices to ensure the quality and reliability of the released software. Here are some best practices to consider when using Maven for release management:

1. **Automate the Release Process**: Automating the release process using Maven and the Maven Release Plugin helps reduce manual errors and ensures consistency across releases. By defining a standardized release process, you can save time and effort in managing releases.

2. **Perform Thorough Testing**: Before creating a release candidate, it is crucial to perform thorough testing, including unit tests, integration tests, and any other relevant tests. This helps identify and fix any issues or bugs before the release, ensuring a stable and reliable release.

3. **Document the Release Process**: Documenting the release process is essential for maintaining a record of the steps involved and ensuring consistency across releases. It

helps new team members understand the release process and serves as a reference for future releases.

4. **Use Version Control System**: Utilize a version control system, such as Git or Subversion, to manage your project's source code and track changes. This allows you to easily revert to previous versions, tag releases, and collaborate with other developers effectively.

5. **Follow Semantic Versioning**: Adhering to the Semantic Versioning scheme helps communicate the nature of changes in each release. By following a consistent versioning scheme, you can manage dependencies effectively and ensure compatibility between different versions of your project.

6. **Monitor and Gather Feedback**: After releasing your project, actively monitor its usage and gather feedback from users. This feedback can help identify any issues or areas for improvement, allowing you to release updates and enhancements in subsequent releases.

By following these best practices and leveraging the capabilities of Maven and the Maven Release Plugin, you can streamline the release management process and ensure the successful delivery of your software to end-users or other developers.

Conclusion

Managing project releases is a critical aspect of software development. Apache Maven provides powerful tools and features to simplify the release management process. In this section, we explored the release management workflow, the Maven Release Plugin, and best practices for managing releases. By effectively managing project releases with Maven, you can ensure the quality, reliability, and timely delivery of your software.

8.3 Using Maven with Java EE Applications

Java EE (Enterprise Edition) is a powerful platform for building large-scale, distributed, and robust enterprise applications. It provides a set of specifications and APIs that enable developers to create scalable and secure applications. Maven, as a build automation tool, can greatly simplify the management and deployment of Java EE applications.

In this section, we will explore how Maven can be used effectively with Java EE applications. We will discuss the benefits of using Maven in a Java EE project, how to set up a Maven project for Java EE, and how to manage dependencies and build the application.

8.3.1 Benefits of Using Maven with Java EE

Maven offers several advantages when it comes to developing Java EE applications:

1. **Dependency Management**: Maven simplifies the management of dependencies in a Java EE project. It provides a centralized repository for storing and retrieving dependencies, making it easy to include external libraries and frameworks in your application.

2. **Consistent Build Process**: Maven follows a standardized build process, which ensures that all developers working on the project have a consistent and reproducible build environment. This helps in reducing build-related issues and ensures that the application can be built and deployed consistently across different environments.

3. **Project Structure**: Maven enforces a standard project structure, which is particularly useful in Java EE applications. It separates the source code from the configuration files, making it easier to manage and maintain the project.

4. **Build Automation**: Maven automates the build process, allowing developers to focus on writing code rather than managing the build. It handles tasks such as compiling the source code, packaging the application, and running tests, saving developers valuable time and effort.

5. **Integration with IDEs**: Maven integrates seamlessly with popular IDEs such as Eclipse, IntelliJ IDEA, and NetBeans. This integration provides features like automatic dependency management, code completion, and build configuration, making it easier to work with Java EE projects.

8.3.2 Setting up a Maven Project for Java EE

To use Maven with Java EE, you need to set up your project correctly. Here are the steps to create a Maven project for a Java EE application:

1. **Create a Maven Project**: Use the Maven command-line tool or your IDE's Maven integration to create a new Maven project. Specify the appropriate archetype for a Java EE application, such as *maven-archetype-webapp* or *maven-archetype-ear*.

2. **Configure the POM**: The Project Object Model (POM) is the heart of a Maven project. Configure the POM to include the necessary dependencies for your Java EE application, such as the Java EE API, servlet API, and any other libraries or frameworks you need.

3. **Set up the Project Structure**: Maven follows a specific project structure for Java EE applications. Place your source code in the *src/main/java* directory, configuration files in *src/main/resources*, and web resources (HTML, CSS, JavaScript) in *src/main/webapp*. Update the POM to reflect this structure.

4. **Configure the Deployment Descriptor**: For Java EE applications, you need to configure the deployment descriptor (e.g., *web.xml* for web applications) to specify the servlets, filters, and other components of your application. Place the deployment descriptor in the appropriate location within the project structure.

8.3.3 Managing Dependencies in a Java EE Project

One of the key benefits of using Maven with Java EE is its powerful dependency management capabilities. Maven simplifies the process of including external libraries and frameworks in your Java EE application.

To manage dependencies in a Java EE project with Maven, follow these steps:

1. **Declare Dependencies**: In the POM file, declare the dependencies your application requires. Specify the group ID, artifact ID, and version of each dependency. Maven will automatically download the dependencies from the configured repositories.

2. **Scope Dependencies**: Maven allows you to specify the scope of each dependency. For Java EE applications, commonly used scopes include *compile*, *provided*, *runtime*, and *test*. Choose the appropriate scope based on when the dependency is needed during the application's lifecycle.

3. **Exclude Transitive Dependencies**: Sometimes, a dependency may bring along its own dependencies (transitive dependencies) that conflict with other dependencies in your project. Use the *<exclusions>* element in the POM to exclude specific transitive dependencies.

4. **Use Dependency Management**: If you have multiple modules in your Java EE project, you can centralize the

management of dependencies by using the *<dependencyManagement>* section in the parent POM. This allows you to define the versions of dependencies in one place and have them inherited by the child modules.

8.3.4 Building a Java EE Application with Maven

Once you have set up your Maven project for Java EE and configured the dependencies, building the application is straightforward. Maven provides a set of build lifecycle phases that you can execute to compile, package, and deploy your Java EE application.

To build a Java EE application with Maven, follow these steps:

1. **Compile the Source Code**: Use the *compile* phase to compile the Java source code in your project. Maven will automatically compile all the source files and place the compiled classes in the appropriate directory.

2. **Package the Application**: Use the *package* phase to package your Java EE application into a deployable artifact, such as a WAR (Web Archive) or an EAR (Enterprise Archive) file. Maven will include all the necessary dependencies and resources in the packaged artifact.

3. **Run Tests**: Use the `test` phase to run the unit tests in your Java EE application. Maven will execute the tests and generate a report with the test results.

4. **Deploy the Application**: Depending on your deployment environment, you can use the *install* or *deploy* phase to deploy your Java EE application. Maven will copy the packaged artifact to the appropriate location, such as a local repository or a remote server.

By following these steps, you can effectively use Maven to build, manage dependencies, and deploy your Java EE applications. Maven's standardized build process and dependency management capabilities make it an ideal choice for Java EE development.

8.4 Working with Maven Profiles

Maven profiles are a powerful feature that allows developers to customize the build process based on different environments, such as development, testing, and production. Profiles provide a way to define different sets of configuration options, dependencies, and build steps that can be activated or deactivated based on specific criteria.

8.4.1 Introduction to Maven Profiles

Maven profiles are defined in the project's POM (Project Object Model) file. A profile is a collection of settings and configurations that can be activated or deactivated based on certain conditions. These conditions can be specified using various criteria, such as the operating system, the presence of certain files, or the value of system properties.

Profiles are useful when you need to build your project differently depending on the environment. For example, you may want to use different database configurations, logging levels, or external service endpoints for development, testing, and production environments. Maven profiles allow you to define these configurations in a centralized manner and activate the appropriate profile based on the environment.

8.4.2 Defining Maven Profiles

To define a Maven profile, you need to add a *<profiles>* section within the project's POM file. Inside the *<profiles>* section, you can define one or more *<profile>* elements, each representing a specific profile. Each profile can have its own set of configurations, dependencies, and build steps.

Here is an example of how to define a Maven profile:

```
<profiles>
  <profile>
    <id>development</id>
    <activation>
      <activeByDefault>true</activeByDefault>
    </activation>
    <properties>
      <database.url>jdbc:mysql://localhost:3306/dev_db</dat
abase.url>
      <logging.level>DEBUG</logging.level>
    </properties>
  </profile>
  <profile>
    <id>production</id>
    <properties>
      <database.url>jdbc:mysql://prod-server:3306/prod_db</
database.url>
      <logging.level>INFO</logging.level>
    </properties>
  </profile>
</profiles>
```

In this example, we have defined two profiles: *development* and *production*. The *development* profile is activated by default (*<activeByDefault>true</activeByDefault>*) and sets the database URL to a local development database and the logging level to *DEBUG*. The *production* profile, on the other hand, sets the database URL to a production server and the logging level to *INFO*.

8.4.3 Activating Maven Profiles

Maven profiles can be activated in several ways. The most common way is through the command line using the *-P* or *--activate-profiles* option followed by a comma-separated list of profile IDs. For example, to activate the *production* profile, you can run the following command:

```
mvn clean install -P production
```

You can also activate profiles based on certain conditions using the *<activation>* element within the profile definition. For example, you can activate a profile only if a specific file exists:

```
<profile>
  <id>custom</id>
  <activation>
    <file>
      <exists>src/main/resources/custom.properties</exists>
    </file>
  </activation>
  ...
</profile>
```

In this example, the *custom* profile will be activated only if the file *src/main/resources/custom.properties* exists.

8.4.4 Overriding Profile Configurations

Sometimes, you may need to override certain configurations within a profile. Maven allows you to do this by using the *<properties>* element within the profile definition. When a profile is activated, Maven will merge the properties defined in the activated profile with the properties defined in the default profile.

For example, let's say you have the following profiles defined:

```
<profiles>
  <profile>
    <id>development</id>
    <properties>
      <database.url>jdbc:mysql://localhost:3306/dev_db</dat
abase.url>
      <logging.level>DEBUG</logging.level>
    </properties>
  </profile>
  <profile>
    <id>production</id>
    <properties>
      <database.url>jdbc:mysql://prod-server:3306/prod_db</
database.url>
      <logging.level>INFO</logging.level>
    </properties>
  </profile>
</profiles>
```

If you activate the *production* profile, the *database.url* property will be overridden with the value *jdbc:mysql://prod-server:3306/prod_db*. However, the *logging.level* property will remain unchanged, as it is not defined in the activated profile.

8.4.5 Using Maven Profiles in Plugins

Maven profiles can also be used within plugins to customize their behavior. Plugins can define their own profiles and activate them based on specific conditions. This allows you to have fine-grained control over the build process and plugin executions.

To use a profile within a plugin, you can use the *<profiles>* element within the plugin configuration. For example:

```
<build>
  <plugins>
    <plugin>
      <groupId>com.example</groupId>
      <artifactId>my-plugin</artifactId>
      <version>1.0.0</version>
      <executions>
        <execution>
          <id>my-execution</id>
          <phase>compile</phase>
          <goals>
            <goal>my-goal</goal>
          </goals>
          <configuration>
            <profiles>
              <profile>development</profile>
            </profiles>
          </configuration>
        </execution>
      </executions>
    </plugin>
  </plugins>
</build>
```

In this example, the *my-plugin* plugin is configured to execute its *my-goal* goal during the *compile* phase. The plugin execution is associated with the *development* profile, so it will only be executed when the *development* profile is activated.

8.4.6 Conclusion

Maven profiles are a powerful feature that allows developers to customize the build process based on different environments. They provide a way to define different sets of configurations, dependencies, and build steps that can be activated or deactivated based on specific criteria. By using Maven profiles effectively, you can streamline your build process and ensure that your project is built consistently across different environments.

8.5 Customizing Maven with Plugins and Extensions

Apache Maven is a powerful build automation tool that provides a wide range of functionality out of the box. However, there may be cases where you need to customize Maven's behavior to suit your specific project requirements. This is where plugins and extensions come into play.

8.5.1 Introduction to Plugins and Extensions

Plugins and extensions are two ways to extend the functionality of Maven. They allow you to add new goals, customize existing goals, and modify the build process to meet your project's needs.

8.5.1.1 Plugins

Plugins are the primary mechanism for extending Maven. They are self-contained units of functionality that can be added to your project's build process. Maven provides a wide range of built-in plugins that cover common tasks such as compiling code, running tests, and packaging artifacts. These plugins can be easily configured and executed using the *<plugins>* section in your project's POM (Project Object Model) file.

In addition to the built-in plugins, there are also numerous third-party plugins available that can be used to perform specialized tasks. These plugins can be easily added to your project by specifying their coordinates (groupId, artifactId, and version) in the POM file.

8.5.1.2 Extensions

Extensions are another way to customize Maven's behavior. Unlike plugins, which are project-specific, extensions are installed globally and can be used across multiple projects. Extensions can modify Maven's core functionality, add new lifecycle phases, or provide additional capabilities.

Extensions are typically packaged as JAR files and can be installed by placing them in the *<MAVEN_HOME>/lib/ext* directory. Once installed, they can be referenced in the POM file using the *<extensions>* section. Maven will automatically load and activate the extensions during the build process.

8.5.2 Using Plugins

Using plugins in Maven is straightforward. You simply need to add the plugin configuration to your project's POM file. The configuration includes the plugin's coordinates, the goals to execute, and any additional parameters required.

To add a plugin, you need to specify its coordinates within the *<plugins>* section of the POM file. The coordinates consist of the plugin's groupId, artifactId, and version. Maven will automatically download the plugin from the central repository or any other configured repository.

Once the plugin is added, you can configure its behavior by specifying the desired goals and their parameters. For example, if you are using the Maven Compiler Plugin to compile your Java code, you can configure the source and target versions, as well as any additional compiler options.

Plugins can be executed by running the corresponding goals from the command line or by using an integrated development environment (IDE) that supports Maven. Maven will automatically resolve the plugin's dependencies and execute the specified goals in the defined order.

8.5.3 Creating Custom Plugins

While Maven provides a vast collection of built-in plugins, there may be cases where you need to create your own custom plugin to perform a specific task. Creating a custom plugin allows you to encapsulate complex functionality and make it reusable across multiple projects.

To create a custom plugin, you need to follow a set of conventions and use the Maven Plugin API. The API provides a framework for defining goals, configuring parameters, and executing the plugin's logic.

The process of creating a custom plugin involves the following steps:

1. Define the plugin's metadata: This includes specifying the plugin's groupId, artifactId, version, and other details in the plugin's POM file.

2. Implement the plugin's goals: Each goal represents a specific task that the plugin can perform. Goals are implemented as Java classes and should extend the `AbstractMojo` class provided by the Maven Plugin API.

3. Configure the plugin's parameters: Parameters allow users to customize the behavior of the plugin. They can be defined as fields in the goal's Java class and annotated with the `@Parameter` annotation.

4. Execute the plugin's logic: The logic of the plugin is implemented in the `execute()` method of the goal's Java class. This method is called by Maven when the goal is executed.

5. Package and install the plugin: Once the plugin is implemented, it needs to be packaged as a JAR file and installed in a Maven repository. This allows other projects to use the custom plugin by specifying its coordinates in their POM files.

8.5.4 Configuring Plugins

Plugins can be configured in the POM file using various elements and attributes. The configuration depends on the specific plugin and its goals. Some common configuration options include:

- Specifying the plugin's version: This can be done by adding the `<version>` element within the plugin's configuration.
- Configuring plugin goals: Each goal can be configured with its own set of parameters. These parameters can be specified within the `<configuration>` element of the goal.
- Binding plugin goals to lifecycle phases: Maven allows you to bind plugin goals to specific lifecycle phases. This ensures that the goals are executed automatically during the build process. The binding can be done using the `<executions>` element within the plugin's configuration.
- Configuring plugin dependencies: If a plugin requires additional dependencies, they can be specified within the `<dependencies>` element of the plugin's configuration.

8.5.5 Troubleshooting Plugins

Sometimes, plugins may not work as expected or encounter issues during the build process. Maven provides several mechanisms for troubleshooting plugin-related problems:

- Verbose output: Running Maven with the `-X` or `--debug` option provides detailed debug output, which can help identify the cause of the problem.
- Plugin-specific documentation: Most plugins provide documentation that explains their usage, configuration options, and troubleshooting tips. Refer to the plugin's documentation for specific guidance.
- Plugin execution order: Maven executes plugins in a specific order based on their configuration. If a plugin is not executing as expected, check its execution order and

ensure that it is correctly bound to the desired lifecycle phase.

- Plugin compatibility: Plugins may have compatibility issues with different versions of Maven or other plugins. Ensure that you are using compatible versions of Maven and the plugins you are using.
- Plugin conflicts: If multiple plugins are configured to perform similar tasks, they may conflict with each other. Review the plugin configuration and remove any conflicting plugins.

By following these troubleshooting techniques, you can identify and resolve issues related to plugins in your Maven build process.

Conclusion

Plugins and extensions are powerful tools for customizing and extending the functionality of Apache Maven. They allow you to add new goals, modify existing goals, and tailor the build process to meet your project's specific requirements. By understanding how to use and create plugins, as well as how to troubleshoot plugin-related issues, you can harness the full potential of Maven and streamline your project's build process.

9. Glossary

Apache Maven: A build automation and project management tool primarily used for Java projects. It uses a Project Object Model (POM) file to manage project dependencies, build processes, and documentation.

Archetype: A Maven template project that provides a basic structure and configuration for a new project.

Build Lifecycle: The sequence of phases that define the steps in the build process of a Maven project, including compiling, testing, packaging, and deploying.

Build Profiles: Configurations in Maven that allow users to customize the build process for different environments or scenarios.

Clean Plugin: A Maven plugin that deletes the target directory containing the built artifacts, ensuring a clean build environment.

Code Coverage: A metric used to measure the percentage of code executed during testing, indicating how thoroughly the tests exercise the codebase.

Continuous Integration (CI): A development practice where developers frequently integrate code into a shared repository, often leading to multiple integrations per day. Each integration is verified by an automated build and tests.

Dependency Management: The process of handling and resolving project dependencies in Maven, ensuring that the correct versions of libraries and modules are used.

Dependency Scope: Specifies the visibility and lifetime of a dependency within different build phases. Common scopes include compile, test, and runtime.

Dependency Version: The specific version of a dependency used in a Maven project.

Integration Testing: Testing that focuses on the interactions between components or systems to ensure they work together as expected.

Javadoc Plugin: A Maven plugin that generates documentation from Java code comments using the Javadoc tool.

Local Repository: A directory on a developer's machine where Maven stores downloaded artifacts and dependencies.

Multi-module Project: A Maven project structure that allows managing multiple related projects under a single umbrella, enabling them to be built and managed together.

Parent POM: A POM file that serves as a template for multiple child projects, allowing shared configurations and dependencies.

Plugin: A component in Maven that provides additional functionality, such as compiling code, packaging binaries, and running tests.

Project Object Model (POM): An XML file that contains information about the project and configuration details used by Maven to build the project.

Remote Repository: A repository hosted on a remote server from which Maven downloads dependencies and artifacts.

Repository Authentication: The process of providing credentials to access a secure remote repository.

Release Management: The process of managing the lifecycle of a project release, including versioning, packaging, and deploying artifacts.

Snapshot: A development version of a project that is still under active development and subject to changes.

src Directory: The directory in a Maven project that contains the source code and resources.

Surefire Plugin: A Maven plugin used to run unit tests during the build process.

Target Directory: The directory where Maven generates and stores the built artifacts, such as compiled classes and packaged binaries.

Transitive Dependency: A dependency that is not directly declared in a project but is included through another dependency.

Unit Testing: Testing individual components or units of code to ensure they function correctly in isolation.

Version Control: The management of changes to source code over time, enabling multiple developers to collaborate on a project. Common tools include Git and Subversion.

Verification: The process of checking that a Maven installation or configuration is set up correctly.

www.ingramcontent.com/pod-product-compliance
Lightning Source LLC
LaVergne TN
LVHW051235050326
832903LV00028B/2414
9798875580550